SINLESS SEX

RECOMMENDATIONS
FOR *SINLESS SEX*

Every person involved in organized religion should read this book. Stayton recounts the challenges and barriers that religious institutions have faced in addressing sexuality in a meaningful and helpful way. It's time for religious institutions to recognize that sexuality is a fundamental aspect of being human and is expressed in many diverse ways that need to be celebrated and affirmed.

—ELI COLEMAN, PhD, Academic Chair in Sexual Health, Professor and Director, Program in Human Sexuality, University of Minnesota Medical School

He's a prophet of pleasure, born on Christmas Day, the best story-telling educator I've seen in action, and a gifted healer of those whose sexuality doesn't fit the confines of Old Time Religion. When Bill Stayton and I met, I was a gay, recovering Catholic who found toxic any references to the Church. There was sexuality and religion, and never the twain shall meet. But, this Baptist pastor's delight in all expressions of one's sexual self, even those I had previously judged as unacceptable, made me a believer not in Church doctrine and authority, but rather in the inseparable link between the intimacy of self and the love of God.

—BRIAN MCNAUGHT, Corporate Trainer on LGBTQ issues and author of *Sex Camp, On Being Gay,* and *Are You Guys Brothers?*

Wearing the hats of both a sexologist and Christian pastor, Bill Stayton in his Sinless Sex *convinces us that we can't reduce the breadth of human sexual diversity to the teachings of act-oriented religions. He understands that the spiritual and the erotic are avenues for meaning-making, and he clearly and concisely challenges organized religions to embrace instead the teachings of pleasure and faith's central premise, love.*

—BEVERLY DALE, DMin, Founder of the Incarnation Institute for Sex & Faith and author of *Advancing Sexual Health for the Christian Client: Data & Dogma*

I recommend Sinless Sex *for the reason the title suggests, that sexuality is not about sin but is as Dr. Stayton so well demonstrates, a natural part of our biological and spiritual world. As he says, "Sexual pleasuring does not hinder spiritual growth; on the contrary, it has great power to expand it." Based on an uncommon expertise in both theology and sexuality, and an appreciation of science, this book can offer to a wide range of people, a wide range of ways of thinking about sexual morality, to their benefit and ours.*

—BETSY CRANE, PhD, Retired Professor/Former Director, Center for Human Sexuality Studies, Widener University

Dr. Stayton's book is full of his personal and professional wisdom and includes the enthusiasm, passion, and compassion that he is known for around the world from his teaching and lecturing. His stories from his career are relatable and jump right off the page as if to come to life. The book is as much a theology, religious history, and life-skills book as it is a primer on the key elements of sexuality that each of us should have in mind every day. He engages the reader in conversation, offering fresh perspectives, wrestling with debates about sex and religion, and posing challenges for readers to take on across the lifespan. Dr. Stayton invites readers to think of themselves holistically and to take a positive sexuality approach to their own life and in their relationships with others, whether they are lovers, friends, or family.

—JUSTIN SITRON, PHD, Associate Professor, Associate Dean, College of Health & Human Services, Director, Interdisciplinary Sexuality Research Collaborative, Widener University

SINLESS SEX

A Challenge to Religions

WILLIAM R. STAYTON

LUMINARE PRESS

WWW.LUMINAREPRESS.COM

Printed in the United States of America

Cover Design by Melissa K. Thomas

Luminare Press
442 Charnelton St.
Eugene, OR 97401
www.luminarepress.com

LCCN: 2020920892
ISBN: 978-1-64388-460-8

To my Family
blessed with the freedom of diversity
and bonded together by unconditional love

TABLE OF CONTENTS

Introduction

To begin, I would like you to get to know me. First, what motivated me to write this book? Over the years I have published many academic journal articles and book chapters on both religion and human sexuality, but given the intensity of interest that so many people have expressed in my work in these areas, I perceived a need to make my writings available to the general reader, the non-specialist. But then, how did I, a minister, get into human sexuality education in the first place? Here is my story.

Early in 1965, while I was serving the First Baptist Church of Gloucester, Massachusetts, my high school youth group asked me if I would offer some sessions on sex education. My feelings were mixed. I felt excited, challenged, scared, and perplexed. I was excited because they were asking for something I did not have the courage to ask for when I was their age, challenged because sexuality is an ethical and moral issue and the church was certainly the proper arena for sex education, scared because I had no idea how the congregation or my community would view such a venture, and perplexed about what I should tell them. What do they need to know? Where would I get my information? Could I be honest, truthful and open with them? What if there was conflict between my answers and their beliefs? Could I lose my job?

I turned to two other clergy in the community, a rabbi and another Protestant minister. Together we decided we would support each other and together offer a four-session course to our high school students. Among our congregations we had about 60 young people. We asked them to bring signed notes from their parents saying they could take our course. We used a current teen sexuality book by Evelyn Millis Duvall, *Facts of Life and Love for Teen-agers.* The night the course began, we had over 400 young people show up—all with signed notes from their parents! We had to move to the sanctuary of the largest of the three congregations. There we were in a sanctuary, under the cross, talking about sex. I must admit it did throw me at first.

The kids were great! I learned more from them during those four weeks than they learned from me. How eager they were to learn! How incredibly incisive were their questions! How sensitive they were to my discomfort! They all returned for the four sessions. There were no discussions about theology. The course was a big hit. Within six weeks, the Board of Education of Gloucester invited me to their meeting and asked if we would offer a course for junior high youth and offered us the high school facilities. For that course, we recruited local Roman Catholic and Protestant clergy to participate and to be small group leaders. I insisted that we offer a concurrent course for parents, who are really the sex educators, both verbally and nonverbally, of their children. Again, we had a large turnout and tremendous success. Other churches and Councils of Churches from communities around Massachusetts heard about our program and asked me to conduct similar programs for them. Soon I traveled to other churches in and out of Massachusetts setting up sex education programs.

It became very apparent to me how hungry people are to know about their sexuality and how strongly our sexuality is influenced by religion.

After my years as a local pastor I obtained a doctoral degree in psychology and counseling at Boston University and became a licensed psychologist. For four years, I served as hospital chaplain at New England Baptist Hospital in Boston and taught human sexuality in their school of nursing. As adjunct faculty at Andover Newton Theological School, I taught pastoral care, including human sexuality. I attended several universities for training in human sexuality and became a therapist and university professor at the University of Pennsylvania in the field of human sexuality education.

During my early years as a graduate school faculty member I helped develop curricula for master's and doctoral degree programs in human sexuality and was a consultant to the Unitarian Universalist Association in the revision of their "About Your Sexuality" curriculum for religious education. We had used this curriculum in training our graduate students to work with religious institutions. The revision of "About Your Sexuality" became "Our Whole Lives" (OWL). Both the Unitarian Universalist denomination and the United Church of Christ have adopted the OWL curriculum.

In 1999, the graduate program in human sexuality at Penn moved to Widener University. Having been the first director there, it has been thrilling to see it grow to now be its own department, with eight faculty and over 250 Master's and Doctoral students. I taught in that program as professor after I retired and learned so much from and with those individuals pursuing degrees in Sex Therapy or Sexuality Education.

After my retirement from Widener, I accepted a professorship at Morehouse School of Medicine in Atlanta. Besides teaching human sexuality courses, I helped develop an Endowed Chair in Sexuality and Religion. After five years I retired from Morehouse.

A comment that I hear very often is "What is a Baptist minister doing in the field of human sexuality? It seems incongruous!" What a sad commentary on the relationship between religion (especially that of Baptists) and sexuality! For example, until recently, most religious denominations denounced persons who identify as lesbian, gay, or transgender. Even worse is a minister who advocates sexual practices often thought as incompatible with religion, such as masturbation, non-marital sex, sex toys, same-sex attraction, and cross-dressing. Actually, the fact is that being a minister in a local congregation led me to this new form of ministry as a sexuality educator and therapist. My story undergirds my belief that we are born both spiritual and sexual. One of the tasks of life is integrating into wholeness these two aspects of our being.

In this book, I would like to share the various ways we can accept, give and receive sexual knowledge and pleasure that I have collected over the years through research and from my own thoughts and experiences in this ministry. I shall offer scriptural, scientific, and cultural contributions which I believe are important to developing an integration of religious belief and the acceptance of sexual pleasure. It is my belief that love, spirituality, and sexuality constitute a natural, integrated whole. We all have the capability to be sexual in the fullest sense of the word—that is, we can embrace our sexuality with affirmation and within our physical and emotional abilities, respond to mutual sexual pleasuring. "God saw that everything that God had made, and indeed, it was very good." (Gen. 1:31).

Religious traditions often separate the sexual from the religious, making people believe they have to either choose to be fully sexual or deeply religious. Did you receive any information or meaning about being a good lover from your religious tradition? This is the dilemma that countless people probably feel all the time. They experience their sexuality, but the meaning they receive from their faith tradition about their sexuality is often harmful or certainly not helpful. It is my belief that everyone is born both spiritual and sexual, but no one is born a good lover. Sexual response is natural; being a good lover is learned. This book attempts to reconcile the two, viewing being fully religious and fully sexual as the real journey to being fully human, using comprehensive sexuality education as a basis for understanding.

The object of this book is to impart useful science-based information about sexuality that will benefit the reader's life, and to correct misinformation about scriptures and religion that the majority of persons from the Abrahamic religions (Judaism, Christianity, and Islam) have been brought up to believe. In view of my background as a minister, family and sex therapist, and professor of psychology and human sexuality, I believe that the themes of this book will be highly beneficial to many readers, especially those still bound by their past religious beliefs. I hope to help people who experience a clash between their religion and their sexuality, and to counteract the false view many people have concerning the biblical view of human sexuality. Then the question becomes: how do we take the information in this book and develop a theology of sinless sex and sexual pleasure that is relevant to real life circumstances?

My own major teachers have been courses taught by sexuality professionals, various books, my students and my clients. Various stories of pain, suffering and healing from sexual ignorance and trauma from my students and clients have been emblazoned on my mind and are embodied in this book. However, care has been taken to preserve the anonymity of all of them.

In part one, I identify how deeply held beliefs can shape our sexual values, whether or not those values are based on science or negative teaching about sexuality and moral development and their impact on one's sexual attitudes and behavior. In part two, the most common current dilemmas regarding sexuality will be covered, especially relating to the different faith traditions. In part three, there is an exploration of possible new directions that can be taken to enrich one's religious practices or spiritual journey based on a theology of sinless sex.

While there are numerous English translations of the Bible, I have chosen to use the *New Revised Standard Version* (NRSV), unless otherwise noted. The NRSV is a version commonly used in Main-line Protestant denominations.

Chapter 1

CULTURAL AND SEXUAL VALUE SYSTEMS: DEEPLY HELD BELIEFS

IN THE LAST 50 YEARS, HUMAN BEINGS HAVE LEARNED more about our sexual behavior and sexual responses than at any time in history. Almost all of this new knowledge is in conflict with, and hence challenges, the extensive history of traditional religious and cultural beliefs. Thus, in order to be helpful and relevant to the sexual concerns of our time, our religious and governmental institutions have to recognize these challenges.

First, from a religious perspective, the major religious focus of sexuality has been its procreative function. "Be fruitful and multiply" (Genesis 1:28) has been the Biblical formula for survival. Since 1850, when the world-wide population was about 1 billion people, a population explosion has occurred. Today, 170+ years later, the world-wide population is nearing 8 billion people. This means our population is growing at a geometric rate and that the biblical formula for human survival has become the formula for human disaster. It has put a strain on our resources, damaged our environment, and burdened our health and welfare systems.

The second new phenomenon that challenges religious proscriptions is the development of contraception, which allows people to protect themselves from either becoming pregnant, or, with the proper use of condoms, getting a sexually transmitted disease. Thus, people can now have sex purely for pleasure, but most religions have not developed a theology that encompasses sex for pleasure and recreation as well as for procreation.

The third new phenomenon is "extended adolescence." In 1850, the average age a child entering puberty was 16 or 17 years. That average has been lowering one year per generation. Today, the average age that a male has his first ejaculation and a female has her first menstrual period is 11 or 12, and it is not unusual to find young people starting puberty at the age of 9 or 10 or even earlier. There are probably many reasons for this phenomenon, but among them are better understanding, and hence care, of fetal development, better nutrition and health care during infancy and childhood, and better national health care in general. Add to this the fact that persons are entering into marriage and having children at a later age, and the result is a greatly extended period of sexual maturity in the absence of the procreational function of sex. In 1850 the average age of marriage was 18 or 19. Today it is 27 to 29. Thus, where adolescence was once a transitional stage between childhood and adulthood lasting some 2 to 4 years, it is now a major stage in human development. Adolescence, or at least the period of time from childhood to marriage, can last some 15 to 20 years. A moral value system and code of sexual behavior that recommended self-control and abstinence until marriage may have made sense when adolescence was a transitional period of 2 to 4 years, but it is not in everyone's interest to make the same recommendation for a 10 to 20 year period. In fact, it could be considered cruel and inhuman, and be a major contributor to later poor sexual satisfaction and sexual dysfunction.

A fourth phenomenon new to human history is that people are living longer. In the early part of the 20th century, the average marriage was 20 to 25 years before one or both partners died, long enough to have children and rear them to adulthood. Today, if a person partners or marries in their mid to late 20s, and stays in that relationship "till death do them part," the average relationship can be 50 years or more. We have not provided the skills to help people live in a long-term relationship and keep it alive, exciting and sexually passionate for 50 years or more.

In exploring these new human phenomena, it is important to understand how one views sexuality and sexual behavior. Some will consider sexual acts as the primary consideration. Others will consider the nature of one's relationships as the central consideration, rather than sexual acts, in making their sexual decisions. Religion and cultural views can also have an important part in sexual decision-making.

Act-Centered Theology

Theological belief systems ask the question, "What does God, or nature, 'intend' for human sexuality?" The first value system, often thought of as being traditional, judges specific "acts of sex" as holding moral or immoral value. This act-centered value system centers itself around the following biblical directive. "So God created man in his own image; in the image of God he created him; male and female he created them. God blessed them and said to them, 'Be fruitful and multiply, fill the earth and subdue it…" (Genesis 1:27-28). The Roman Catholic Church developed a belief system based on this scripture and made it Canon Law in 1918. The same belief system is held by many Jewish, non-Catholic Christian, and Islamic communities.

The view holds that the key to understanding God's "intention" for sexuality is that male sperm is the basis of life itself, since it is through the sperm that life continues to the next generation. Hence, the purpose of the female sex was thought to be the ground in which the sperm (or seed) was planted. In the beginning there was no knowledge of ova being necessary for the propagation of life. The role of the female was only to be supporter and nurturer of the male's sperm. It does not matter what science and research now say, according to Genesis, since these roles were fixed by God.

This view has had enormous political, religious, and economic implications throughout recorded history. According to this belief, the male is superior and male sperm has two purposes. The first is to procreate. Sperm has no other functional use. One does not urinate better because of sperm, nor does it keep one from illness. The second purpose is more subtle, but just as important. With the commandment to "be fruitful and multiply" and sperm playing the first vital role, it was easy for men to impregnate as many women as possible. This led to the importance of having a structure for the upbringing and education of children, as it would be irresponsible to just go around planting one's sperm at random. It followed that this in turn should form the framework for the need for marriage and the family. Marriage provides a context of responsibility associated with life-giving sperm.

Clearly, this system is based on male sexuality, which in turn defines the role of males in society. They are its leaders. However, women also play important biological and social roles. They are the biological supporter and nurturer of the sperm and thus their role is also to be the supporter and nurturer of the male. Procreation, however, requires sexual intercourse with a person of the opposite sex, but only in an appropriate context. The context is believed to be marriage of one man and one woman. This view was obviously developed before other forms of conception were developed, such as in vitro fertilization (IVF), Intrauterine insemination (IUI), donated sperm, eggs, or embryos, etc.

This paradigm for human sexuality is overtly a part of the Canon Law of 1918 of the Roman Catholic Church and, tellingly, of most of the world's major religions as well. Moreover, it goes even further in that it stipulates what emphatically is not acceptable in sexual behavior. If male sperm is for procreation, then birth control, abortion, and same-sex marriage are not allowable. If sperm-based procreation requires sexual intercourse, then masturbation is not allowed. In this view, if a male's sperm requires another person, then the fetishes and bestiality will not be allowed. If male sperm requires sexual intercourse with another person of the opposite sex, then homosexuality, bisexuality, and transsexuality will not be allowed. If male sperm requires sexual intercourse with another person of the opposite sex, then it must be in an appropriate manner. Thus, for the purist, oral sex, anal sex, and many of the erotic positions for sexual intercourse, as well as sex toys, would not be allowed because these do not result in procreation. Some theologians even claimed that the "missionary position" (or man on top) is the only position for sexual intercourse that God would approve. After all, since sperm is often called man's seed, one plants seed downward, not upward or sideways.

To summarize sexual value system "A", the focus of concern is on "Sexual Acts" in determining what is allowed or not allowed, reinforced by calling these acts moral or immoral. The location of authority is external, such as God, holy scriptures, parents, and religious authorities. An outside body proclaims moral responsibility, often represented by a person who is detached and aloof. The purpose of this value system is to maintain tradition and authority and therefore the social order. The reward is divine favor and heaven.

Regarding sex education, the above system advocates "abstinence until marriage," which fosters ignorance, secretiveness, and trauma. "Abstinence until marriage" is the official government-sponsored sex education program in the United States. Within this program, authorities value ignorance because they fear that knowledge about sex will encourage sexual acting out and promiscuity. They value secrecy because youth are not encouraged to ask specific questions about sex, such as any about masturbation, sexual behaviors, homosexuality, abortion, contraception, safer sex, or condom use. If they do, they may receive negative, disapproving or even fear-inducing responses. Consequently, trauma may occur because, whereas sexual feelings and curiosity are natural to human beings, this value system discourages discussion about almost all sexual behavior, except that which promotes procreation within the context of marriage between a man and a woman. Guilt and shame are the result of allowing other sexual thoughts, fantasies, or questions if they are not related to marriage and procreation. Even sexual intimacy in marriage for pleasure or fun is sometimes questioned. Whenever sex is seen as a "duty," this results in greatly diminished fun and pleasure.

The following is an example of this theology, which could equally well have been put forward by a conservative Protestant theologian. It was in a news report of Pope John Paul II's letter to the bishops of the Roman Catholic Church regarding homosexuality:

> Homosexual tendencies ... are 'ordered toward an intrinsic moral evil, and thus the inclination itself must be seen as an objective disorder' ... The Vatican letter said that the church position 'cannot be revised by pressure from civil legislation or trend of the movement' ... Bishops must state clearly that homosexuality is immoral and resist pressure from the pro-homosexual movement within the church to change its teaching ... Bishops 'should keep as their uppermost concern the responsibility to defend and promote family life' (*Philadelphia Inquirer*, 10/31/86, 1-A).

Relationship-Centered Theology

At the other end of the theological spectrum is a sexual value system based on relationships. The answer to the theological question, "What does God (or nature) 'intend' regarding sexuality?" would be that human sexuality is intended for relationships. Relationships are what the Bible, creation, God, and life are all about. A relationship-centered theology says that there is nothing inherently immoral or evil about the acts of sex. The important issues regarding sex are the motives and consequences of the act(s). This theological belief system is just as ancient, just as "biblical," and has had just as many "moral" spokespersons throughout history as act-centered theology. The Bible, in relationship-centered theology, is seen as the history of human beings' relationship to self, to others (both male and female), to God, and to one's possessions and resources. The central focus of the biblical message was well stated by Jesus when he was asked what the most important commandment was in the law. He responded by quoting his Bible from Leviticus 19:18 and Deuteronomy 6:5 "'Love the Lord your God with all your heart, with all your soul, with all your mind.' That is the greatest commandment. It comes first. The second is like it: 'Love your neighbor as yourself.' Everything in the Law and the prophets hangs on these two commandments." (Matthew 22:34-40).

For relationship-centered theology, trying to identify a specific idea about an act of sex in the Bible is to misread the biblical message. The responsibility of religion, therefore, is to help individuals, families, and society to develop criteria for healthy decision-making regarding sexual matters, taking into account the motives and consequences of sexual acts. There is nothing inherently moral or immoral about any of the acts of sex as long as the act is freely chosen between or among participants, without any coercion, or the causing of harm to participants or relationships. The purpose of our engaging in sexual acts is to help us to grow as individuals, couples, families, and indeed, even as a society. The reward for this kind of decision-making regarding sexual acts is that life itself is lived more meaningfully and responsibly in the present, as opposed to rewards in life after death.

A good spokesperson for this theology was Pope John XXIII. He opened minds in the Roman Catholic Church and started a movement that is still strongly felt in our world. He started the ecumenical movement that led to dialogue with other faith communities, both Christian and non-Christian. He suggested taking a new look at the issues surrounding sex, and it resulted in an excellent textbook entitled *Human Sexuality: New Directions in American Catholic Thought* (Kosnik et al, 1977). This textbook, commissioned by The Catholic Theological Society of America, questioned many, if not most, of the sexual behaviors which were not allowed and traditional considered to be immoral.

To summarize, the relationship-centered sexual value system holds that both God's creation and the scriptures contain teaching about the nature of relationships, teachings that great religious leaders, like the Hebrew prophets, Jesus, and/or Mohammed, all promoted. The focus of this value system is on one's relationship with God, with self, with others, and with such things in our life and environment as material possessions, money, and justice. This value system teaches that all of society is involved in the moral climate, that moral values promote growth of better people and therefore of a better society. Thus, the reward for holding responsible sexual values is the creation of a better, more meaningful life in the here and now.

Age-appropriate comprehensive sex education would foster this sexual value system and would result in responsible sexual behavior, since much sexual acting out by adolescents reflects simple curiosity. Furthermore, when questions are answered without producing guilt and shame, young people are encouraged to put more thought into their sexual decisions and behavior. Because this value system encourages communication about sexuality, further questioning is encouraged. Sexual issues such as masturbation, homosexuality, contraception, abortion, safer sexual practices, and condom use are explained as natural and are not condemned. Decision-making skills are often taught and practiced. Premarital, extramarital, or alternative sexual lifestyles are seen as personal decisions. Gay, lesbian, bisexual, transgender, intersex persons, and persons with a disability are fully accepted and affirmed as sexual beings. Marriages are formed between people in a loving relationship and they do not rely on partners fulfilling particular roles, nor do they necessarily have to be between a male and a female.

Most Common Sexual Value System: A Matter of Confusion

Unfortunately, most people fall somewhere between these two theological systems, which becomes the third sexual value system. It derives from both the first and second value systems depending on the issue and comfort level with the "act," but it often becomes confusing, because there is no consistent theological or scriptural basis for it. For example, a person may accept masturbation, contraception, and oral sex from a relational value system because it enhances their relationship with self or others, but may reject abortion, homosexuality, and anal sex because of the theological teachings, or simply as a result of discomfort with these practices.

Some religious institutions may operate from a "don't ask, don't tell" or a "love the sinner, hate the sin" philosophy. Hence, religions holding this third value system might be negative toward premarital sex, extramarital sex, homo-sexuality, and same-sex marriage, but be silent, or give limited approval, to such practices as masturbation, non-marital sex between consenting adults, abortion, and/or safer sexual behaviors.

As we look at the world's major religions, one may see how these three sexual value systems are reflected in each of them. Act-centered theology may be proclaimed and taught, but when it comes to one's most private and personal decision-making system, a relationship-centered theology seems more relevant and "right." Since the two systems are not compatible, however, conflict results. An example of such conflict is provided by a family (father, mother, and 13-year-old daughter) who came to see me. The father told the following story.

Their daughter, who had just turned 13, was pregnant. It was against the family's act-centered belief system for her to have an abortion, but as they talked, searched their hearts, and prayed about the matter, they finally made a decision that an abortion was the best solution. He said several factors influenced their decision. The first consid-eration was the daughter's age. Second, she was a brilliant student and had a promising academic future. Third, she did not know who the father of the child was because she had had consensual sex with five boys at the same time. This was before the era of DNA testing. The family felt that going through the pregnancy and having the child would deeply hurt her future. The father then told me that the decision had been even more difficult and complicated because he was very active in the "Right-To-Life" group in his community. He said that he believed in the views of that organization with all his heart and he wanted to continue in his leadership capacity, but that when it came to making the decision regarding their own daughter, the "Right-To-Life" (act-centered) value system was just not relevant to their personal circumstances. Because it was what the daughter really wanted, I supported the final decision of the family for her to have an abortion and even made the arrangements for the procedure through our local Planned Parenthood affiliate.

As hypocritical as this family may sound, my heart went out to them because they were caught between two incompatible sexual value systems, one act-centered, the other relationship-centered. Proponents of one system believe they are right, that they are moral and biblical, and that the other is wrong, uninformed, immoral, and unbiblical.

My parents were both brought up in acts-based churches in Ohio. My father was a Methodist, my mother was a Baptist. After marriage, they moved to the West Coast, left any involvement in a church, believing it was truly irrelevant to their life. The only church experience I had as a child was attending Christmas Eve services to hear the music and Easter Sunrise Service in our local community. As an adolescent, I decided to join a church, much to my parents' disappointment. The church was definitely an acts-based church. While I liked being a part of that community, the theology made no sense to me. In discussions with my parents, they would call the theology "baloney." I am forever thankful for their attitude because they made more sense to me than did my church. When I went to college, I took a religion course that was totally based on a relationship-based theology. Over that semester, I felt that religion and spirituality began to make sense to me and were in line with what I learned from my parents. As I continued my career in religion, psychology and human sexuality, a relationship-based theology made so much sense to me and became the basis of my work as a pastor, chaplain, therapist, and professor of sexuality.

I very frequently see individuals who are caught in this conflict between an act-centered sexual value system and a relationship-centered system. As hard as people may try, the two systems cannot be reconciled or integrated without appearing to be hypocritical. That is simply one of the ambiguities of being human.

Chapter 2

OUR MORAL
DEVELOPMENT

HISTORICALLY, THE FAMILY AND OUR RELIGIOUS INSTITU-
tions have had the task of being the moral teachers and
purveyors of behavioral values for the family and society.
Although morality can be learned early in the family, it can
also be instinctual, based on religious teachings or acquired
from outside the family and religion. It is a lifelong process.

The question is, however, where does morality come
from? Is it nature or nurture or both? According to Jonathan Haidt (2013), in his book *The Righteous Mind* some
are nativists who believe our morality comes from nature.
The belief is that "moral knowledge is native in our minds."
Morality is in our God-inscribed hearts through the Bible.
Darwin believed our moral emotions evolved in our brain
development. Other moralists believed that our moral
development came through nurturance, like John Locke,
who believed that our brains were more or less blank slates
at birth. Because morality varies around the world and
across the centuries, it is hard to believe that it is innate,
but rather derives from observation and experience. I
believe morality can be developed both through nature

and nurture, that is, through a set of evolved intuitions and learned through applying those intuitions within a particular culture. Haidt believes that "we are born to be righteous, but we have to learn what, exactly, people like us should be righteous about" (pg 31).

In this chapter, there will be a consideration of all of these factors in exploring the educational process in both sexual expressions and religion. These factors may be applicable to understanding the interface between sexuality and religion around the world.

India and the Beginning of Modern Sexuality Education

As a speaker at the 1st International Congress on Life Span Sexuality Education in India (January 2007) I found it was the perfect country to study the interface between sexuality education and religion. India is such a contrast of cultures and religions, marriage and family customs, and of ancient and modern history.

India is particularly relevant to understanding the interface between sexuality and religion because in India one finds all the major religions of the world: Hinduism, Judaism, Christianity, Islam, Sikh, and Buddhism. It is also where, according to tradition, sexuality education began with the Kama Sutra (2nd Century, C.E.). The Kama Sutra explores and teaches how to be a good lover to oneself, outside of marriage, in same sex relations, in heterosexual relationships, in group sex, and explores oral sex, anal pleasuring, sadomasochism, and the use of toys. While furthering the naturalness of sexual expressions in those early periods of history, that time is in stark contrast to the repressed forms of sexual expression that I learned about in talking with both ordinary citizens and sexuality professionals in India today. The introduction of conservative Muslim and European colonial Christianity in India in the last century brought about the development of strict purity regulations regarding morality and proper sexual practices and relations. Thus young people in today's modern world are caught in a clash between the sexual conservatism of their parents and grandparents and the modern world of freer sexual expression not unlike what their ancestors may have experienced.

Two poignant experiences in India piqued my interest in further pursuing this subject of morality and religion. The first was in Khajuraho, a town of many temples, some of which joyously celebrate life and erotic sexuality through massive sculpture portrayals. I have a photo of a young couple in one of the temples, with their two children, standing in front of a huge wall of erotic sculptures of various sexual positions and configurations of people. I wondered how this young Indian couple, brought up in India's sexually repressive culture, would answer their children's natural questions: "What are the people doing?" "Why are they doing these things?" "Do you and Mommy/Daddy do these things?" "Why are these in this temple?" Great questions for inquiring young minds! These are natural questions and provide an exciting and challenging opportunity for positive and healthy sexuality education. Informing children about sexual behavior among adults does not promote sexual acting out. Too often parents have the belief that knowledge promotes immoral and irresponsible sexual behavior. There is no scientific basis to this belief system. The evidence shows that accurate and honest knowledge promotes appropriate and responsible sexual behavior.

The second experience was meeting two young adults very much in love and who had secretly been meeting, almost daily, for five years. They asked to meet with me for my counsel regarding their story. They met at the university and their families did not know about their relationship. They were members of two different religions, Hindu and Sikh, both with similar strong morally based premarital sexual restrictions. The taboo for such a relationship was so strong that their families, some friends and their faith communities would disown them if they knew about this relationship. They both felt strongly about their own religion and were also pulled by the force and depth of their love. There was no interest in converting to the other's religion, but both believed that their children, if they had any, would benefit from both religious traditions.

I have known many couples—Christian and Jew, Catholic and Protestant, Muslim and Christian, Hindu and Jew—who have experienced the same dynamic as this young couple in India. I have also known many unhappy marriages which were entered into in order to please their family's or religion's requirements. It is this clash of sexual morality and love with family and religious tradition that tear at the fabric of human relationships.

What are all the factors that go into the decision-making in these types of scenarios? What do we know about both sexual and religious development that informs this decision-making? To answer these questions we must, first, normalize the issues, so that the mixed-religious couple can discuss their relationship with their families without shame or guilt. Second, providing some knowledge about where their parents, friends and religious community are coming from can be very helpful. Finally, helping them to develop the skills and a strategy for approaching parents, friends, and religious community is necessary. This book is designed to address these three recommendations.

Sacred Scripture and Moral Sexual Behavior

Judaism, the Torah and the Hebrew Scriptures—Jewish tradition cannot be characterized as simply affirming or repressing the erotic. Some texts have positive views of sexual pleasure, some have limits on the variety of sexual expression. In the Torah (the first five books of the Hebrew Bible) God is described in masculine terminology. There are no sexual organs or female counterpart. The relationship between God and Israel is described as a desexualized marriage. Men are God's spouse, women are invisible. There were many restrictions. Before the commandments were given to Moses, Israelite men were ordered not to engage in sexual relations three days prior to the woman's period. Semen and menstrual blood were seen as polluted. Also forbidden by the Torah is masturbation, same gender sex, sex with animals, sex with women who are menstruating, family members related by blood, and sex with someone considered to be property of another man. Interestingly, neither prostitution nor multiple wives is forbidden. This was a privilege of patriarchy.

The Talmud, which consists of discussions and debates about the Torah, was written around 500 C.E. It portrays a complex attitude towards sexuality. The Talmud debates were deeply concerned with how to control sexual passion, which was necessary for procreation but potentially dangerous if not controlled. While procreation was a positive value, pleasure was seen as a necessary dimension of marriage. Any sexual activity was seen as acceptable, including anal or oral sex and even women on top if it produced pleasure for her.

Marriage was also complex. Scholars have identified many patterns or forms of marriage in the Hebrew Bible. Jacob, Moses, and Samson are examples of being in a matriarchal marriage, where the children carried the mother's name. Jeremiah, and later Paul in the Christian testament, advocated a patriarchal marriage where the woman was considered property and was totally under her husband's control. Abraham, Jacob, and David were in polygamous marriages, which were the most common among marriage styles in the Bible. Monogamy was neither prescribed nor proscribed in the Hebrew scriptures. There are examples of marriage being restricted to one's own religion or kinship, while other examples, such as Esau, Joseph and Moses married outside their religion or culture. The Bible even has examples of incestuous relationships and marriages, such as Abraham, Isaac, Judah, and Onan.

Regarding male pleasure, masturbation was strictly forbidden. Men should control sexual desire through study and prayer. Semen was considered holy and therefore could not be spilled (Genesis 38). It was believed that women lacked the discipline and intelligence to control their desire, thus it was the man's responsibility to have all the control. Women were not to be trusted. In present day in Judaism only the strictly orthodox Jews still hold to these beliefs. Even today, Hebrew males are taught to pray daily: "Blessed art Thou O Lord our God, King of the Universe, who has not made me a woman."

The control of sexual practices, especially for women, was in place in Judaism and was further embedded in the developing cultural and religious traditions of the first few centuries in the C.E. Sexuality and spirituality were well on the way to total separation and thus ready for the complete repression introduced by Greco-Roman Christianity.

Christianity and the New Testament Scriptures—The development of Christian sexual practices in the first few centuries of the C.E. was influenced by two major forces: Hebrew history and traditions, and the sex-negative, fearful belief system and practices of Greco-Roman syncretism, which fostered a body/soul dualism (Lawrence, 1990). One either followed the lustful pleasures of body sexuality or the richer life of the spiritual or soul. Marriage was for procreation only and sexual pleasure was disdained. Spirituality and sexual practices were enemies. While Jesus was not affected by this dualism, Paul certainly was, as he lived, traveled, and struggled with the Greco-Roman worldview. The unequal marriage between the Hebrew form of Christianity, which was basically sex-positive and the Christianity that developed out of the Greco-Roman syncretism was finalized with St. Augustine (425 C.E.), which was built on his belief that sexual desire was the original sin in Genesis of being thrown out of the Garden of Eden. The result was shame and guilt based in sex-negativity. Purity was related to virginity and sexual abstinence (Greenblatt, 2017). The split between sexuality and spirituality was cemented in the *Summa Theologica* of the sexual purist Thomas Aquinas in the 13th century.

Over the centuries the Roman Catholic Church developed a long list of the forbidden sexual practices: masturbation, abortion, artificial birth control, sterilization, in vitro fertilization, homosexual behavior, bisexuality, transgender expression, premarital sex, extramarital sex, divorce, same gender marriage, and any of the alternative sexual lifestyles. Roman Catholic Theology also defined the role and subjugation of women in the church and society.

Celibacy, chastity, and sexual purity became cardinal virtues. Sexual shame and guilt became the cardinal sin. Sexual sin and all of the above prohibitions resulted from the New Testament scriptures, not the non-Christian philosophies. A contemporary experience of this sex-negative theology is documented in Linda Kay Klein's book, *PURE: Inside the Evangelical Movement that Shamed a Generation of Young Women and How I Broke Free* (2019). Sexual sin was not a part of the gospels' or Jesus' teachings, nor do the gospels say anything about sexual practices. Jesus' emphasis was on the nature of relationships.

The crack in the Roman Catholic teachings about sexuality came with reformers, such as Luther and Calvin in the 16th century followed by many others. Today, just in North America, there are 1200 different Christian denominations, including Roman Catholic, Eastern Orthodox, historic Protestant denominations, Evangelical, Pentecostal, and Racial/Ethnic denominations, and many independent churches. Even within the Roman Catholic Church in America there are organizations that speak out against traditional teachings of their church: Catholics for Choice (1973), Women's Ordination Conference (1975), Call to Action (1976), and Voice of the Faithful (their motto is "Keep the Faith, Change the Church") (2002).

Protestantism and Scriptures—According to the *World Christian Encyclopedia* by Barrett, Kurian, & Johnson (Oxford University Press, 2nd Edition, 2001) there were over 31,000 distinct Protestant denominations in 238 countries. Thus it would be impossible to cover a view of sexuality and sexual behavior that would do justice to either the religion or to sexuality. Christianity, however, is the one world religion that I have found developing sexuality education curriculum for its members. Later in chapter 10 , we will explore how sexuality education in the major Christian denominations in the United States has been helpful or not helpful in preparing youth and adults to meet the sexual and spiritual/religious integration necessary for finding meaning to the sexual issues faced by humans in today's world.

Islam and the Qur'an—Islam began in the Arabian peninsula in the 7th century C.E. with the prophet Muhammad, who received the revelation of the Qur'an, the Muslim holy scripture. While Islam accepts both the Hebrew and Christian scriptures to some extent, the final revelation from Allah (God) is found in the Qur'an. Like Judaism and Christianity, it is a patriarchal religion. Sexually, there are a lot of mixed messages between the Qur'an and Muhammad's life. Islam was not influenced by the Greek, Roman, and Stoic philosophers and their negative view of sex and the body. There is no original sin or sexual sins for disobeying Allah, no sexual shame or guilt. The concept of celibacy (not to marry) is a foreign issue and not an acceptable choice in Islam. Men are expected to marry. Sensuality and sexuality are celebrated, but within the framework of marriage.

Marriage and sex are complicated in Islam. Muhammad is reported to have had fifteen wives. After the death of his first wife, fifteen years his senior, he married fourteen more females. His favorite wife, A'isha, was only six years old when he married her, although it is believed that he did not have intercourse with her until she was nine or ten. It was a long marriage and he died in her arms.

The major revelations about sex in the Qur'an are as follows: Sexual practices and behaviors that are permitted or lawful are masturbation, birth control, abortion with strong restrictions, oral sex, polygamy, genital intercourse, and divorce with conditions. The sexual practices and behaviors that are prohibited or unlawful are: anal intercourse, intercourse during menses, adultery, homosexuality, lesbianism, bestiality, rape, child molesting, incest, obscenity, nudism, orgies, open marriage, fetishes, sado-masochism, enjoyment of pornography, necrophilia, celibacy, and castration (al-Qaradawi (1984), ch. 3).

Moral Sexual Behavior in Historical Context

A problem that has to be faced is that acceptable moral sexual behavior has differed throughout history. A few examples that I have found in the literature are from Judd Marmor's (1994) *Psychiatry in Transition*, ch. 7.

During the first century of the Common Era in parts of the European continent,

- Public nudity was accepted;

- Virginity was not prized;

- Extramarital sex was taken for granted;

- Frank and open sexuality was the rule;

- Incest was frequent;

- Women were open aggressors in inviting inter-course; and

- Bastardy was a mark of distinction.

During the Feudal era from the 9th to the 15th century,

- New brides were often deflowered by a Feudal Lord;

- In some societies, all wedding guests would copulate with the bride;

- Guilt about sexuality became a cardinal feature of western life and religion;

- Celibacy, chastity and virginity were exalted and were considered of higher moral value than non-virginity;

- Coitus was sanctioned only for procreative purposes;

- Laws were ordained against abortion—laws which had not existed among Greeks, Romans or Jews;

- Sexual intercourse between married couples was illegal on Sundays, Wednesdays, and Fridays, as well as 40 days before Easter and Christmas and from time of conception to 40 days after birth.

- This was in contrast to Islamic law, which considered it grounds for divorce if coitus did not take place at least once a week.

Repressive societies enforced cruel sanctions to regulate

sexual taboos. An epidemic developed of sexual patholo-
gies such as rape, whipping oneself or another, hysterical
possession by witches and devils, phantom pregnancies, etc.
In contrast, in societies in which the expression of sexuality
was open and guilt-free, such as in parts of Europe prior to
the Middle Ages and in what were then considered "primi-
tive" societies, the so-called sexual violences were much
less frequent. Homosexual behaviors of the early Greek
and Romans were not exclusively homosexual, but part of
a pattern of bisexuality in which homosexual feelings were
accepted as being as natural as heterosexual feelings. Actually, the ideals of romantic love and marriage for love are
relatively late developments in Western history and did not
begin until the 12th century of the Common Era.

Thus, we find that there is nothing about our current
sexual attitudes, practices, and deeply held beliefs that can
be assumed to be sacred or unchangeable. They have clearly
been subject to much change and evolution in the past and
will undoubtedly be different in the future.

Moral Dilemmas in Sexual Decision-Making

The question is: How do we understand our own moral
development? How do we help our children to be sexually
healthy and express responsible sexual behavior, especially
in this time in history of moral relativity? I found Harvard
psychologist Lawrence Kohlberg helpful in defining the
moral stages of development in his study of male youth.
There are three broad categories in the description of moral
development: pre-conventional, conventional, and post-
conventional, with two stages in each for a total of six stages
of moral development. Kohlberg believed that persons go

through these stages in sequence, although a person may get stuck at any one stage of development and stay there even for a lifetime. He believed that a person cannot skip any stage (*The Psychology of Moral Development*, 1981).

At the pre-conventional level, stage one involves a punishment and obedience orientation to moral issues. Activities are good or bad, right or wrong. The moral judgments are made by an authority and are not to be questioned. There is no moral reasoning, only obedience because of the fear of consequences. Phrases like "abortion is always wrong" or "masturbation is a sin" are examples of beliefs strictly held to in stage one because the authority said so and obedience is important lest one be punished. However, it is not unusual to find a stage one person who will have an abortion or masturbate if there is no possibility in their mind that they will be caught. They may have to struggle with their guilt and shame at some point, and a person with a bisexual or homosexual orientation may have a particularly difficult time with self-acceptance and lifestyle options. Our religious institutions also reflect the above stages of moral development. As we saw in the last chapter, some religious institutions reflect an act-centered value system. They demand obedience and punishment as the consequence of disobedience. This is true in any fundamentalist institution, whether Jewish, Christian or Muslim.

Stage two denotes a more hedonistic perspective. A person sees that there are so many different types of value systems that they just have to "do their own thing." This person is out for their own interest, although they may be against unfairness and injustice, and decisions are self-centered, based more on an "I'll scratch your back, if you scratch mine" mentality. There is little responsibility or loyalty to relationships. The adolescent might say "I'll have sex if I want, because I think I can do whatever I want regardless of what my parents or religious teaching says." A resultant pregnancy would be seen as an inconvenience, and thus an abortion would be the answer without any real moral conflict.

Thinking in stage three adheres much more to conventional mores. The adolescent's reference group of family or religious group provides the standards of conduct and behavior to which the person holds. A major issue is being a "nice/good girl" or "good/nice boy." If the reference group says it is best to be a virgin because nice girls are virgins and do not fool around, the person will hold to that value. Another stage three decision would be an adolescent couple, who out of passion have sex. If the girl becomes pregnant, there might be the feeling that they are no longer pure or clean, but they will take responsibility for that pregnancy by deciding to get married, have an abortion, or continue with the unmarried pregnancy. They may experience lifelong guilt and shame for their actions.

Stage four decisions are in line with conventional standards with more of a focus on what is acceptable in the peer group rather than family or religious community. For example, an adolescent female and/or male may believe that all the other kids their age are sexually active, so a "good girl" or "good boy" might also become sexually active when they are "in love." A person would condone sex for those young adults who can handle the consequences if a pregnancy does occur by getting married, caring for the child as unmarried parents, or having an abortion. Decisions are made in line with conventional standards with more of a focus on law and order. To be responsible, one must follow the rules of society or of one's particular religious institution or peer group and accept the consequences of one's actions.

There are also many faith communities associated with stages 3 and 4, where there is conformity to and maintenance of the moral conventions expected of a family, group, or religion, regardless of the consequences. There is also a sense of law and order focusing on the rules of the social order so that society can function smoothly. When issues that challenge conventional ideas, such as masturbation, sex outside of marriage, or homosexuality arise, the concept of "don't ask, don't tell" is often recommended. As seen in the last chapter, religions often exemplify the mixed act-centered/relationship-centered value system, which has little basis in any systematic theology.

The post-conventional level of moral development, according to Kohlberg, is built around the concepts of justice and ideals. In stage five, there is a flexible procedure for establishing codes of conduct. In this stage, a major theme might be that the law regarding sexual behavior needs to be flexible as long as there is no harm being done. There would be an emphasis on the agreement between or among the individuals involved. If two adolescents mutually agree to have sex and take on the responsibility to see that they do not get pregnant or are willing to handle the consequences of a pregnancy, premarital sex is considered right. Anything between consenting adults that is done without coercion and is out of sight and sound of unwilling observers is acceptable as long as it does not cause harm. The person in stage five would consider homosexuality, masturbation, premarital sex, and abortion to be matters of individual conscience and preference rather than a matter of law and order or religious concern.

Finally, in stage six, there are universal ethical principles a person strives for that are self-chosen and would be based on universal principles of justice, equality, reciprocity, and the dignity of the individual. This involves, for some, a universal God based upon the above universal principles. In stages five or six, in any faith community, Jewish, Christian, Muslim, or other, the individual may define his or her own moral decisions apart from authoritative figures or scriptures. It is believed that there can be bad laws or misleading scriptures. Laws can also change to meet the demand of social change. For some, the last stage of moral development is that of universal ethical principles, a view based on a relationship-centered sexual value system. Clearly a person's own conscience becomes important in moral decisions.

Humanism is an example of this final level, emphasizing critical thinking, devotion to human welfare, and a life centered on human values. Current religious denominations that embody this view are the Unitarian Universalist Association (UUA) and the United Church of Christ (UCC). These values are taught in their sex education curriculum, *Our Whole Lives* (OWL). The curriculum of OWL is based on seven principles:

- All persons are sexual.

- Sexuality is a good part of the human experience.

- Human beings are sexual from the time they are born until they die.

- It can be natural to express sexual feelings in a variety of ways.

- People engage in healthy sexual behavior for a variety of reasons, including to express caring and love, to experience intimacy and connection with another, to share pleasure, to bring new life into the world, and to experience fun and relaxation.

- Sexuality in our society is damaged by violence, exploitation, alienation, dishonesty, abuse of power, and the treatment of persons as objects.

- It is healthier for young adolescents to postpone sexual intercourse.

The curriculum has a companion activity and resource guide, *Sexuality and Our Faith*, which supports sexuality education in a religious context. (www.UUA.org/re/owl)

Understanding Moral Development in Religions

Haidt (2013) has an interesting definition of moral systems that can also be helpful for understanding moral development and decision-making, as well as in conflict management. "Moral systems are interlocking sets of values, virtues, norms, practices, identities, institutions, technologies, and evolved psychological mechanisms that work together to suppress or regulate self-interest and make cooperative societies possible" (pg. 313).

Haidt (2013) defines morality by what humans do, rather than specifying what the system's content counts as moral. Thus, belonging to a religious institution involves both believing and doing. He also believes that morality can both bind and blind humans in their moral decision-making. For example, in orthodoxy there is a focus on belonging, and their morality is based on some form of binding where once a person, book or principle is declared sacred, one can no longer question its legitimacy. On the other hand, liberalism constitutes the ability to care about things beyond oneself and to bind oneself into belonging only to groups that pursue larger projects. Traditionally, conservatives see radical change as dangerous and thus need structures and constraints, including laws, institutions, customs, traditions, nations, and religions in order to thrive. Whether orthodox, conservative or liberal, one can also be blind to what the other offers. Thus, liberals, who have done so much to bring about freedom and equal opportunity, often do not provide sufficient structure or constraints that lead to stability.

But do we not need both, that is: religions of order and stability together with religions of progress and reform? Every religious institution "is exposed to two opposite dangers: ossification through too much discipline and reverence for tradition, on the one hand; on the other hand, dissolution, or subjection to foreign conquest, through the growth of an individualism and personal independence that makes cooperation impossible." (Haidt quoting Bertram Russell, 2013, p. 344). Although morality can both bind and blind, there is a need to pursue and organize around science-based and universally-sound moral sexual rights. I have attempted to provide this type of moral development and decision-making in this book.

In the following chapters, we will examine contemporary issues related to sex and biology, gender identity, sexual orientation and alternative sexual lifestyles in the context of religion.

Chapter 3

SEXUALITY AND BIOLOGY

Evolution vs. Creation

How can we apply some of the more abstract ideas in the previous chapters to contemporary real life conflicts and dilemmas that exist at the intersection of religion and sexuality? Perhaps it is best to start at the very beginning—i.e., with creation itself. The Bible is not a biology book nor a book about biology, but many in the Abrahamic religions (Judaism, Christianity, and Islam) have used the Bible as their source of biological knowledge about creation. One of the most commonly cited passages from the Bible is Genesis 1: "In the beginning when God created the heavens and the earth".... that God created sea life, then birds, sea monsters, cattle, and wild animals. God then created humankind, male and female, to have dominion over all life that had been created.

But this is not the only version of the creation story that the Bible offers. In Genesis, Chapter 2, there is an alternative version where God created the heavens and the earth and man "from the dust of the ground," and then planted a garden, Eden. Then God created sea life, the animals and birds. This was not enough, so God caused a deep sleep in the man and, according to scripture, took one of his ribs and made a woman. "This at last is bone of my bones and flesh of my flesh; this one shall be called Woman for out of Man this one was taken" (Genesis 2:23).

Well-established scientific facts show that both Genesis stories of creation, as well-loved as they are, are biologically completely false. They are evolutionarily and biologically impossible. Evolutionary theory, rather than "biblical mythology," teaches that everything evolved from sea life through amphibians to mammals, apes to humans (Homo sapiens), and from female as the primary sex to male as the secondary sex. In Genesis, we read that life evolved through the male, not the female.

The question then is how do we define "what is a female and what is a male?" In this chapter, you will learn the answer to this question is not simple to answer. Humans are not just female or male! While there is a developmental sequence for each sex, the answer is not that humans are either a female or a male, but rather a myriad of possibilities in between. In fact, the way humans develop between female and male is on a continuum. This story of human development that follows is fascinating!

Over the millennia since those biblical stories were written down, science has taught us so much about how human beings develop. Being a male or female is more than having a penis or vagina; there is a whole series of developments in embryonic and fetal development, from chromosomal to gonadal to hormonal to internal genitalia to external genitalia. In fact, it is not until the sixth week that an embryo differentiates as male or female, depending on the chromosomal arrangement. First of all, the female always has an X sex-determining chromosome while the male has both X and Y sex-determining chromosomes. If both parents contribute an X sex-determining chromosome (XX), the child will be a female. If the male contributes a Y chromosome (XY), the child will be a male. So we could define a female as one with XX chromosomes and a male as one with XY chromosomes. However, at conception, this is not yet obvious.

But that is not all that happens. About the fourth or fifth week, gonadal tissue appears in the developing embryo, which can become either ovaries and produce eggs, or develop into testicles and produce sperm. Next, the ovaries or testicles manufacture hormones. Despite their obvious biological differences, both ovaries and testicles produce all three sex hormones: progesterone (pregnancy hormone), estrogen (female hormone), and androgen/testosterone (male hormone). The differences are the result of proportions in the mixture. In every developing fetus, there are two sets of internal genitalia, known as Mullerian (female) and Wolfian (male). Mullerian internal genitalia become a uterus, fallopian tubes, and vagina; the Wolfian internal genitalia become a prostate, vas deferens, and seminal vesicles. The same external genital structure will become either a clitoris or penis. The internal and external genitalia develops based on the message given by the body's XX or XY chromosomes. Essentially, we begin as forms without a determined biological sex, and eventually develop different sexual organs and anatomies. Rather than Genesis's story of Eve being created from Adam, science teaches that the female internal and external genitalia are the "default" and the male Y and androgen have to be added to both shut down female development and encourage the development of male internal and external genitalia. This fact is a profound negation of the message of Genesis, patriarchy, and the many religious systems dominated by males!

Science does not need to negate one's amazement of the wonders of creation or faith that an unknown intelligence that some know as God started it all.

Intersexuality

Variation is at the root of all things biological, so it is no surprise that differences can occur all along the developmental pathway. This has been referred to as Intersexuality and more recently as Disorders or Differences in Sex Development (DSD). These terms replace previous labels such as hermaphrodite. According to the World Health Organization (WHO), statistically around the world, one out of every 2,000 live births develops with differences in sex development in such a way that the person may be considered to be intersex. Such differences may be related to chromosomes and/or hormones and affect genital and reproductive anatomy as well as sexuality and fertility. They may be mild or more significant. A fairly common example of a mild DSD is hypospadias, which is when a male's urinary opening is not at the tip of the penis but instead on the side. Some people may never know they have such variations; others become aware when they do not menstruate if labeled female or are unable to create a pregnancy. Some are identified at birth, such as when a baby is born with what appears to be a large clitoris or a "micro penis." "Intersex individuals have the condition of either having both male and female gonadal tissue in one individual or of having the gonads of one sex and external genitalia that is of the other sex or is ambiguous" (Merriam-Webster).

Following are some examples of intersexuality that both clergy and therapists may find in their congregation or practice.

There are many different types of chromosomal anomalies. While the mother always contributes an X chromosome to an offspring, it is possible, for example, that the father does not contribute any sex-determining chromosome at all (X0). Thus the child can only be a female. This female, however, may have some distinguishing characteristics: she may be very short (probably not over 5 feet tall), may have webbing between her toes or fingers, little neck flexibility, and will be infertile. This condition is known as Turner's Syndrome. According to the World Health Organization (WHO), one out of every 2500 live female births is a Turner's Syndrome individual.

I once had a brilliant graduate student, short in stature, who was married and knew that she and her husband would have to adopt children if they wanted to have a family. As a young teenager, she did not develop height, breasts, or menstruation. Her pediatrician said she was a "late bloomer." When she started college, she still had not developed breasts or started menstruation. She found out from her college medical clinic that she had Turner's Syndrome and was started on female hormones in order to develop her secondary sex characteristics. She developed naturally, but learned that she would be unable to bear children. She and her husband decided to adopt a child. She had a strained relationship with her mother, because her mother felt her daughter's condition was God's punishment to her for "sexual sins" that she had committed before her daughter's birth. Her mother believed the biblical verses from Exodus 20: 5 and 34:6-7 that the "Lord….by no means clear the guilty, punishing for their parents' sins their children and their grandchildren, as well as the third and the fourth generation." Unfortunately her mother could not be convinced otherwise, even though those same passages speak of God's forgiveness for those who repent their sins.

Another chromosomal pattern is XXY (Klinefelter's Syndrome). The child is male, but may also show some differences from "normal." He will often be tall, infertile, and may have difficulty in establishing good, close relationships. According to WHO, approximately 1 in 700 live male births is someone with Klinefelter's Syndrome. Many males do not know that they have this syndrome. I have treated several in my therapy practice. They often experience work, marital, or fertility problems. Therapy, along with good medical treatment and advice, can be very helpful and lead to successful outcomes. Clergy with a good understanding of the various genetic differences can also be very helpful as a support in gaining healthy outcomes.

In working with clergy around sexual matters, I have found it helpful for them to have the above information in order for them to understand and be helpful to members of their congregations who have this diversity in their families. This knowledge has provided much discussion both about the theological implications of the above differences and pastoral approaches to working with individuals and families.

Several years ago, I had a family referred to me because it was thought that their young 12 year-old son might be a transsexual. He had started to cross-dress when he was four years old and did it every day. I noted two things about him. One was that he was very short and had not yet started through his pubertal changes. The other was that he had very few friends and that this had always been true. His only consistent playmate was his younger sister. Over a period of about one and a half years, he went through a variety of ideas about who he was including being transgender, cross-dresser, having same-sex interest, and heterosexual interest, only to find that he could be any of these possibilities. I tried to normalize all of his sexual interests listed above.

I finally requested a chromosomal test for him and he was examined at Johns Hopkins University adolescent gender clinic. He was discovered to have a XYXO chromosomal mosaic. The analysis was that he is susceptible to the whole range of sexual differences and lifestyles. This condition is now known as Noonan's Syndrome. His pastor and church were not helpful to the family at all, because everything the boy went through was considered immoral and sinful and not within the church's value system. The family felt lost and alone; their only tie to religious acceptance was through me, a former pastor. Although I worked with him for a year and a half to normalize his behavior and understanding, he decided that he was not a transsexual. He liked his genitalia and did not want to change. He decided to give up his cross-dressing because it no longer was an interest, although he knew it would be okay for him to take it up later if he wanted. While he claimed for a period of time that he was gay, he had no interest in having a same-sex sexual experience, but he knew that it would be okay to be gay. Then he met a girl in his class that he started dating and told me he was heterosexual. The great part of this story is that his parents were always accepting of all his options. They just wanted him to be happy and well-adjusted. During this time, I referred the whole family to a family therapist that I had trained. The family therapy was successful based on a follow-up with the therapist several years later. I tried to meet with his family's pastor to help him understand Noonan's Syndrome and how he could be helpful to the family, but he had no interest, so the family left their church.

Not only can there be different chromosomal patterns, but other differences may also occur during fetal development. For example, in an otherwise XX female fetus there can be an overdose of the male hormone, androgen (testosterone). A possibility is that instead of a clitoris, the child develops a penis. Years ago, a family came to see me because they were told they had a boy at birth because he had a penis. They reared him as a boy and he was very active in sports. At the age of ten he began to develop breasts. The doctor told the family he had gynecomastia and could later have surgery. He had undescended testicles which they were told would descend to his scrotum when he got older. Then he began to have breakthrough bleeding in the scrotal area which turned out to be the beginning of a menstrual period. At this point the family learned that they really had a daughter and the doctors told them the best thing for their child would be to have a hysterectomy and mastectomy and to treat him with male hormones to aid in the development of male secondary sex characteristics. Today some doctors would recommend differently and suggest therapy to help the young person make the decision.

There can also be varieties of androgen insensitivity in male fetal development; that is, the fetus may have XY chromosomes, but when the internal and external genitalia begin to develop, an insensitivity to the male hormone causes the fetus to develop as female. The child is reared as a female, but because of her XY chromosomes, she will never menstruate or get pregnant. She may need some estrogen for female secondary sex characteristics to develop normally and she may have to have surgery to lengthen her vagina.

I knew a mother of an XY daughter and had her speak to my graduate students every year. When her daughter was born she was told that she had a boy, although her son had a mini-penis which meant nothing to her. Six weeks later, she was told by an endocrinologist that she really had a girl and that her medical team suggested that the child undergo surgery to shorten the penis and make a vagina. There were several surgeries and a lot of emotion involved with the mother, who had bonded with her son. She says that she had to accept that her son had died, but her daughter was doing very well. Her daughter grew up confused about her sexual identity, which was more male than female. She was drawn to stereotypically boy toys and wanted to be a police officer or a firefighter when she grew up. She was often angry or depressed to the point of being suicidal throughout her childhood and teen years. What this mother and her child wanted to do was educate doctors, clergy, teachers, and parents about her issues so that other children would not go through what she had experienced. She told her child if she wanted to transition to male, her parents would totally support her. Her father was also very involved in this process, although I never met him personally. Today adults who have DSD have organized that no surgeries be performed until the child is old enough to decide for themselves what gender and what body they want to have.

The parents had been church members in the same community since they were children, but they left the church after the surgeries on their daughter because they believed they would never receive any acceptance or support from any church community for their actions. Several of these parents in therapy felt they received no help or understanding from a pastor in making a decision whether or not to have surgery or help in normalizing their child's genitalia and relieving their shame and guilt about their anatomy. Normalizing the idea of variant genitalia was so important in all the clients I had, so they could make an informed decision on what they wanted to do about having any genital reconstruction.

Having a religious community and clergy supportive of the process and decision-making is such an important and helpful factor in working with families of intersex children. Helping clergy to understand these types of biological differences has been very helpful in their working with congregants with understanding and relieving them of any shame or guilt.

There is also a condition known as "bladder exstrophy." It is estimated that world-wide 1 in 20,000 to 50,000 live births will have this condition (http://www.urologyhealth. org/urologic-conditions/bladder-exstrophy). Generally, the bladder and genitalia have not developed and are outside the abdominal wall in the newborn child. The rest of the newborn is normal in appearance and results from a full-term pregnancy. There are only a few hospitals throughout the U.S. that can treat such children. While I was on the faculty of the University of Pennsylvania, which has one such hospital, I was called in as a consultant regarding the sex education of these children. The hospital had periodic meetings with their families. The issue was whether or not the surgeons should form female genitalia on these children in spite of their chromosomal pattern. The surgeons would tell the parents "it is easier to make a hole, than build a pole." They would then advise the parents to raise their child as a female with a female name, toys, and activities, even though some of these XY children had bonded as males with their parents and had lived for weeks and months as males.

This had created huge behavioral problems in many of the children, whose parents were told not to tell them of their chromosomal differences. As sex educators, we had a different view. We advised the doctors that any further surgeries should match a child's chromosomal gender, and that there should be sex education for the whole family, including that the child should be educated to understand their developmental issues truthfully. This last was deemed necessary because our counseling center provided support- ive therapy for many angry teenagers and young adults who had been ignorant of their condition. For more informa- tion see the website: Association for the Bladder Exstrophy Community.

So what, once more, is a male and what is a female? As you might suppose at this juncture, there is no simple answer. Early on in my experience with students, therapy clients, therapists, doctors, and administrators, I began to recognize the importance of the sexual values systems that inform decision-making, especially about sexuality and sexual behaviors. When families have children born with any of the above conditions, whether their religious belief systems will be helpful depends on whether their religious belief system is an act-centered or relationship-centered system. In the case of these biological differences, the act- centered theology will most often look at the parents as the cause of the child's differences, which will not help them to psychologically and spiritually adjust to these differences.

"The Lord God...punishes the iniquity (sins or wickedness) of the parents upon the children and the children's children to the third and fourth generation." (Exodus 34:7 New English Bible)

A relationship-centered theology, on the other hand, would want to know more about the conditions and to understand them, so that one's faith community could be more supportive of the person in relation to self, family and future. Unfortunately, most parents and their clergy do not know about these biological anomalies. The salient point is that we are all different, and it is healthier for all when we appreciate our differences. Hence, the biological education of parents, doctors, health care workers, and clergy is a matter of great importance! For more information see https://interactadvocates.org/resources/intersex-organizations/

Now we move from one's biological development to the other components that go into human development. These components are gender identity and expression, sexual orientation, and lifestyle decisions. It is also important to note that the following chapters explain separate developmental issues. Too often, both professionals and the general public merge them together and this only confuses our understanding of human development. We now turn to the development of gender identity and expression.

Chapter 4

GENDER IDENTITY AND EXPRESSION

THE SUBJECT OF GENDER HAS GROWN LARGER AND MORE socially and politically complex today due to the visibility and advocacy of those who are transgender or non-binary, meaning those whose gender identity is different from the gender they were thought to be at birth. Transgender is an umbrella term that includes many ways of being and seeing one's gender on a spectrum. I begin this chapter with a story from my own professional history. Here I refer to people who cross-dress or identify as transsexual. People who cross-dresser are individuals who find meaning in dressing part time in the clothes that are stereotypical of the other gender. Generally, they do not want to change their sex. Today many prefer to call them bigender persons. Transsexuals are persons who live as another gender, whether or not they decide to have hormonal treatment or surgical intervention. Today many call themselves binary or transgender persons.

In the mid-1980s, a couple made an appointment to see me. The issue was that the husband was a cross-dresser. The wife did not have any problem with it, but they wanted to know how and when to tell their pre-pubertal twin children, a boy and a girl, about their father's cross-dressing. They had no shame or guilt about the cross-dressing and had made it a fun part of their marital relationship. Their concern was that if they waited until the children went through puberty, it could affect their own identity concerns. I agreed that it would be best to either tell them before puberty or when the children were in their late teens. They decided to tell them before puberty because it would be a good educational experience and he would not have to hide his cross-dressing any longer. The children were fine with their dad's cross-dressing with the following restrictions. First, if cross-dressed and going out in the car, she would enter the car in the garage so the neighbors would not know. It is important to note that most cross-dressers prefer, when they are cross-dressed, to be referred to in their cross-dressed gender. Second, that he would not cross-dress if any of their friends or their children's friends were coming over. On the other hand, his daughter was very excited about going shopping for women's clothes with her dad and acting as his fashion consultant.

After the process of telling their children was over, the couple approached me with another problem. The husband, a PhD nuclear engineer by profession, said he knew of no other men who cross-dressed, but guessed that there must be others like him. I suggested that he advertise in local papers and invite them to a meeting. I volunteered my office as a safe space for such a meeting. The first night, they had 13 men show up. Each month they met, more attended. By the time a year had gone by, there was an average attendance of over 100 cross-dressers and male-to-female (MtF) trans-sexuals each month. Most were married, but for many their cross-dressing was done in secret from their wives. A group for FtM transpeople met at another time of the month.

The group called themselves Renaissance Educational Association and had an office in our space, and now after 30+ years, Renaissance is still meeting (See http://ren. org/). At each meeting, they have an orientation to the organization, AA meetings, spouses' meeting, transsexual meeting for MtF members, a different monthly speaker might present make-up tips, a fashion show, how to dress creatively, hormone therapy, voice therapy, trans surgery, or spirituality.

They chose the name of Renaissance Educational Association because they saw themselves as a transitional movement marked by humanistic values. Their missions included educating the public, students and religious communities about transgenderism, as well as providing support for transgender persons. The word spread about this organization through ads in the gay news, therapists, word of mouth, PFLAG, and journal reporters from local papers. At one time there were over 750 members in the greater Philadelphia, New Jersey, and Delaware area with an average attendance each month of 100.

I was asked to speak several times and was always moved by the spiritual concerns of the group. None of them perceived their church or synagogue as being open to learning about the phenomenon of cross-dressing or bi-gender or transgender. Thankfully, transgender acceptance is changing for some churches and synagogues and a few denominations as they become discussed more in the general public. Unfortunately, there is still strong opposition among most, but not all, evangelical clergy and churches, and Conservative and Orthodox Judaism as well as Islam and Hinduism. Historically, most indigenous cultures were accepting of bigender and transgender persons, until Christianity intervened.

I mention this story because Renaissance, now known as Renaissance Transgender Association, is quite a unique offering that may be absent from other towns and cities. Yet its membership shows the prevalence of differences in gender identity and expression. This has become a subject of discussion in the wider culture, and is often hotly debated. You may ask: What do we know about this transgender phenomenon? Is there a difference between being transgender and cross-dressing or bi-gender? Does it affect both sexes? The answer is yes, it affects all genders. It has led to a rejection of the idea that there are just two genders, and what is now called the gender binary.

In summary, transgender is an umbrella term and includes both cross-dressing or bigender, non-surgical transgender and pre- and post-surgical transgender. Individuals who cross-dress like wearing clothes that are considered feminine (if they are male) or masculine (if they are female), but cross-dressing may be for fun, for eroticism, and relaxation. Female cross-dressers tend to cause less controversy because it is more acceptable for women to have a "male" hair style and wear men's garments, including suits and ties. People who are transgender but have not had surgery are those who do not want to change their sexual anatomy, but may live in their daily lives as the other gender. Some people who are transgender are those persons, both male and female, who do not identify at all with their birth gender, and have had their sex and possibly their name changed legally.

Sex and Gender

After the birth of a child, a sex is assigned to it and it is reared accordingly. When the person delivering the baby says, "it's a boy or a girl," a whole series of events takes place. One study of delivery room procedures found that girl babies are held closer to the nursing personnel and parents' bodies, while boy babies are held at length from the body and jostled more vigorously, and boys are talked to louder while girls are talked to in a softer voice. Then a name is added, as well as colors signifying whether it is a boy or girl, and then there are girl toys and boy toys. All of these things have an impact on the child's developing identity from the earliest age. Finally, the child's own behavior helps to define them as male or female. The child usually, but not always, identifies either as a girl or boy. There are parents today who do not use either gender stereotypical names or toys; this is one of many cultural changes. We do not know all the reasons why some children grow up to be gender neutral or transgender.

Everyone has a sex, gender identity, gender expression, and sexual orientation. While each of these are different and distinct concepts, they are also connected in a number of ways. Understanding what different terms mean is very important. It is also important to use accurate language, so that we are all talking about the same thing when discussing topics of sexuality. Terms can also be complex and confusing, and culturally variant, so it is not always possible to know all the appropriate language. Some people use the letters LGBTIQQAA (meaning lesbian, gay, bisexual, transgender, intersex, questioning, queer, asexual, and ally) in different configurations, so the following is some basic information which may be helpful. It is also important to note that these terms are always evolving, with new terms being created and others changing in meaning. Geographical areas may have different terms. I live both in California and Pennsylvania. Terms and their meanings can be different in different communities. For example, I was recently speaking in Missouri. Being queer had a negative connotation in that area of Missouri, as opposed to its positive meaning in San Francisco and Philadelphia. This is also true throughout the world. Terms had different meanings when I was in Scotland, India, or China.

Biological Sex: A person's "sex" refers to one's anatomy, chromosomes, etc., that identifies a person as male or female—although, as the reader has already seen, it is not as "clear cut" as one might think, as someone may be intersex.

Intersex: This is a general term used for a variety of conditions in which a person is born with a reproductive, sexual anatomy, chromosomal, or hormonal difference that doesn't seem to fit the typical definitions of female or male, such as mixed genitalia, internalized genitalia, ambiguous genitalia, etc. Intersex anatomy doesn't always show up at birth, but may when "they" (now considered an acceptable term for either singular or plural uses) reach the age of puberty, or find themselves to be an infertile adult. Some people are born with subtler forms of sex anatomy variations, some of which won't show up until later in life or never unless there is an autopsy.

Gender Identity: the sex with which a person identifies in their own head and heart. This refers to psychology; the gender that one identifies as applying to them, such as male, female, gender neutral, gender non-binary, transgender, etc.

Cisgender: a person whose gender identity matches their biological sex assigned at birth.

Transgender: According to the American Psychological Association "Transgender is an umbrella term used to describe people whose gender identity (sense of themselves as male or female) or gender expression differs from socially constructed norms associated with their birth sex. This includes androgynous, bigendered, and gender queer people, who tend to see traditional concepts of gender as restrictive" (apa.org/Guidelines for Psychological Practice with Transgender and Gender Nonconforming People, December 2015).

Genderqueer: a person who identifies as neither a woman or a man or may identify as a combination of both. Some use other terms, such as non-binary, genderfluid, gender non-conforming.

For some, the words "sex role" and "gender role" are often used interchangeably. This can be confusing. I find it more helpful to separate them. Sex role has to do with biologically different roles between male and female. Gender is more about the social and cultural identification and expression of male and female, masculine and feminine. There are really only four differences in the sex role of male and female. Only females lactate (secrete milk), gestate (carry a pregnancy in the uterus), and menstruate (have a period). Not all females lactate, gestate, or menstruate, but it is the female sex role. Males impregnate (produce sperm). Although not all males produce sperm, it is the male sex role. Everything else is negotiable, and is thus referred to as the gender coding of masculine and feminine attitudes, feelings and behaviors.

Gender Coding

At one time the Gender Identity Clinic of John's Hopkins University believed everyone goes through a process of coding masculine and feminine attitudes, feelings and behaviors. Those attitudes, feelings and behaviors that one codes as appropriate for their own gender will code positive (+). Those that one codes as appropriate for the other gender will code negative (-). There may also be a coding of flexibility (+/-).

In the illustration at the top of the next page, flexibility is where the circles overlap. According to Merriam-Webster Dictionary, flexibility is defined as "yielding to influence and characterized by a ready capability to adapt to new, different, or changing requirements."

In recent years gender coding has radically changed from being socially simplistic to being complex. For one thing equality between men and women is becoming more real and the time in which we live in 2020 is very transitional. The model of gender coding has been helpful in the past to explain attitudes, feelings, and behaviors to students and therapy clients. I think it worth reviewing because it may help explain the divisiveness in society today.

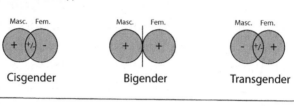

Stayton, The Gender Spectrum

Identification (+)
Complementation (-)

Cisgender   Androgynous   Bigender   Transgender   Transgender

With the male as an example (although it could just as well be a female), we can see from the illustration on the top left the way coding generally takes place. For example, let us say that a traditional or cisgender male codes washing dishes as negative because he believes it is a female coded role. This means that throughout life he will have to go against his nature to wash dishes, even if he is a dishwasher by vocation. It will never feel right to him. Let us say, however, that he codes washing dishes as positive (+). This means that he will want to do dishes because it will feel right to him. He may not even have to be asked to do dishes. But let us say that he codes washing dishes in the flexible area. This means that if he partners with a person who feels that housework should be equally divided, he will do fine with washing dishes. On the other hand, if he partners with a traditionalist who never wants their partner to put his hands in dishwater, he will do fine in that relationship also.

It is important to note that over the past 50+ years, the coding of attitudes, feelings, and behaviors has radically changed, in that more children and youth are coding in the flexible area, so that they are more comfortable with a wide variety of attitudes, feelings and behaviors and there is little absolute coding. The conflict is often between generations. What the parents and grandparents may have coded as absolute, their children and youth are coding as flexible.

For example, my step-father coded short hair or crewcuts for males. In fact, he was a veteran and had a crew-cut all his adult life. In the 1970s, when our sons grew their hair down over their shoulders, he could not stop commenting each time we saw him that we were raising our sons to not be masculine enough. He had coded short hair as positive and long hair on males as negative. Our sons were being consistent with their peers. My step-father could never make that adjustment. The fact is that more men and women today are entering vocations, doing activities, and even wearing clothes that were once coded as gender-specific.

In the middle of the gender spectrum is the person who codes both masculine and feminine as positive and there is no area of flexibility. This is a cross-dresser or bigender person. Some bigender persons have to fantasize or cross-dress in order to be sexually aroused. Others who cross-dress may be doing it for fun, enjoyment, and eroticism, but can also be sexually aroused in their birth gender. For some bigender persons it may be difficult or even seem impossible to change. In that case it is best for the obligatory bigender person and their partner to adjust to this fact or they'll fight it all their lives. There should be no pathology placed on bigender persons or cross-dressers for any reason. There are also those who do not identify with either masculine or feminine and consider themselves as non-gendered. All the above are part of gender development and should be considered normal.

The right side illustration in the gender spectrum is a person who may either identify as transgender or transsexual. This person codes opposite to their birth anatomy. We do not always know the reason; there are several good theories. The classical statement is for the person to say that they have always known that they were born into the wrong body.

For the person who is brought up in a religious household, they will often pray from very early on that they will wake up the next morning in the body of the other sex. It is as if God perpetrated a cruel hoax by having them in the wrong body. Such a person may undergo a sexual affirmation process, possibly including surgery, because it is easier to alter the person's body and not possible to alter their mind to correspond to their body. Some transmen opt for only "top surgery" by having their chest masculinized. Whether or not they have surgery, many use hormone therapy, which can have a dramatic effect on how one looks and feels. Others do not choose either surgery or hormones but instead dress in a way that is gender neutral or non-binary.

A recent development is identifying one's pronouns. For example, my pronouns as a cisgender man are "he/him/his." A cisgender or transgender woman might say "she/her/hers." Those people who identify as gender non-binary or gender non-conforming may use "they/them/theirs." Some may want to use a non-specific term like "ze" as an example. It is a matter of respect and sensitivity to use the pronouns that people prefer.

I once had a transgender client identified as male at birth and reared as a boy who went through 20+ years of psychoanalysis, several times a week, and in the end still felt she was a female. At age 63 this patient finally had gender affirmation surgery. She had been married three times before the surgery and certainly tried to accept being a male. She was a Quaker and came from a Quaker Meeting that had a relationship-centered theological stance. She believed that the only thing that brought her through surgery alive was her Quaker faith and support. Several years later when she died, I attended her Quaker funeral and I was very moved to hear testimony after testimony of how much she had meant to the life of her Quaker meeting as she went through the gender transition. Her former wife was a member of the same Quaker Meeting and women's group and spoke lovingly on her behalf, as did her surgeon.

To complicate the matter of sex and gender even more, I have a colleague, a surgeon, who is a transwoman. When she was a man, he saved his sperm. Several years later, as a woman, she married another woman and they decided to have a child. She used the saved sperm to impregnate her partner. They had twins, a boy and a girl. The transwoman took hormones to help her lactate, thus both could nurse the twins. Both women are the biological parents of the twins. They went on Oprah Winfrey's TV show and shared their story. Following a divorce, my trans friend married another woman and they also became parents of a child, conceived from the saved sperm. Other couples are going through the same process in order to become parents. How might you explain these stories to your family, friends, schools, and faith communities?

It is easy to see that the religious organizations that follow an act-centered theology would have great trouble with coding differences, thus making psychological adjustment at best, difficult, and at worst, impossible. Act-centered theology would say it is not right to tamper with

God's creation. The only biblical reference that addresses this phenomenon is: "No woman shall wear an article of man's clothing, nor shall a man put on woman's dress, for those who do these things are abominable to the Lord your God." (Deuteronomy 22:5). Given what we know about the origins of the Bible and the ever-changing attitudes to sex and gender, these prohibitions belong to an ancient society, not to ours.

Transgender individuals who come from an act-centered theology have to supersede the mandate not to tamper with what God gave them in order to explore gender issues. I am constantly amazed at how many transpersons have a very deep faith in God. While they often come from an act-centered theology, they feel deep in their hearts that there is a loving God who accepts them and wants them to be whole as a person in the other gender. It is this faith that carried them through their years as a child, adolescent, and then adult.

Relationship-centered theology would take into account what the medical community has learned from scientific research about gender development and gender roles and expression and would do best to help that person make a healthy adjustment to their gender role and expression regardless of sexual anatomy.

As illustrated in this chapter, human sexuality has no simple binary divisions when it comes to gender identity. Everything is on a spectrum. This absence of binary divisions will continue to be illustrated in the chapters that follow. We will next turn to the development of sexual orientation, which also exists on a spectrum that is non-binary.

Chapter 5

SEXUAL ORIENTATION: WHAT TURNS US ON

ONE OF THE MOST CONFLICTUAL AND MISUNDERSTOOD areas in human sexual development is sexual orientation. Heterosexuality? Homosexuality? Bisexuality? Autosexuality? In America's sexually repressive culture where many people view sexuality from a pathological model, homosexuality and bisexuality or any of the above have often been considered sick and sinful. Heterosexuality, as regulated by many religious traditions under rigid conditions and with major qualifications, is usually viewed as healthy and redemptive. Sexual relationships are only considered healthy with one person of the opposite sex, with intercourse only permissible after marriage and often preferably in one position (the man on top), with the understanding that if it is enjoyed it is because it fulfills the real purpose of sexual intercourse— procreation. For some, limited foreplay is on the "approved" list as long as it does not include self-stimulation, oral-genital lovemaking, anal lovemaking or fantasies of anything other than the spouse and present situation. By the time individuals, who have received these messages, become sexually mature, sex can often seem exciting, fearful and disgusting.

Fortunately, all of the concepts listed above are being challenged. Experience, feelings, knowledge, and common sense have all proved the rigid conditions and major qualifications to be misguided. Many people cannot imagine their parents or grandparents experiencing sexual freedom. When I bring this up in my classes, students cringe trying to imagine their elders having wild sexual experiences. The reaction of students, often said with disgust, can be, "Yuck, not my parents or grandparents!" Attitudinal change is often slow and sometimes painful. With so many people living in various alternative lifestyles and with all the discussion and controversy regarding sexual orientation, it is important for all of us to be aware of the latest research into, and theorizing about, eroticism and sexual orientation.

Unfortunately, in the religious sphere, many are still asking questions about what causes homosexuality, usually for the purposes of disapproval and/or intervention. I believe that, given our present state of knowledge, this question is no longer appropriate. In our day, being lesbian or gay is more visible than in the past. In the 1970s and beyond, I started as a clergy to officiate at gay weddings in a church, even though it was not legally recognized. I married them in the eyes of God. My wife and I also served as surrogate parents for many people who had been disowned by their family.

Most persons either have gay family members, gay neighbors, gay work associates, or gay church members. Gay persons are prominent as news anchors, in movies, as journalists, politicians, teachers, clergy, and business owners. Gay Pride parades are held in many of our cities. Every Protestant, Roman Catholic, Jewish, and even Muslim religion has a gay advocacy group, although most are not approved by their denomination. Those religious organizations, so far, that are accepting of gay people are: Unitarian Universalist Association, United Church of Christ, Disciples of Christ, Episcopal, and some Presbyterian and Lutheran Associations, a few Roman Catholic dioceses, and Reformed, Reconstructionist, and some Conservative Jewish congregations.

Many people talk in terms of opposites: hot or cold, sick or healthy, male or female, dead or alive, homosexual or heterosexual, and so forth, as if we had sharp dividing lines between differences. Yet we know there are no absolutes in the human experience; everything is viewed within a context. Experience demonstrates that reality exists along a spectrum between imagined absolutes. The same is true of the concept of sexuality.

One of the early sex researchers, Alfred Kinsey, and his associates at Indiana University saw sexual orientation on a seven point bisexual continuum between exclusively heterosexual and exclusively homosexual, based on experiences and/or fantasies with other persons.

FIGURE 1.   THE KINSEY SEXUALITY SCALE

Exclusive heterosexuality	Predominant heterosexuality with incidental homosexuality	Predominant heterosexuality with more than incidental homosexuality	Ambisexuality	Predominant homosexuality with more than incidental heterosexuality	Predominant homosexuality with incidental heterosexuality	Exclusive homosexuality
0	1	2	3	4	5	6

Source: McCary, J.L. *Human Sexuality* 3rd ed. (New York: Basic Books 1971) p. 339.

Based on their research, Kinsey believed that a 0 (zero), or exclusively heterosexual person, would be one who never had any type of genital homosexual experience, desire or fantasy. A 6 (six), or exclusively homosexual person, would be one who never had any type of genital heterosexual experience, desire or fantasy. In between these two extremes would be gradations of homosexual and heterosexual experiences, desires or fantasies.

Almost any college textbook on Human Sexuality has information on the results of Kinsey's study on sexual orientation based on 5300 men and 5900 women in the late 1940s. Probably there is no more than 10% at either end of the continuum, with the majority of people on a bell-shaped curve being between 1 and 5 on the Kinsey scale. Researchers from Freud to Kinsey to Masters and Johnson (the famous sex therapy researchers from Washington University in St. Louis), agree about the bisexual potential of the majority of people. In fact, there is no research to indicate that humans are born to be either 0 or 6 on the Kinsey scale. To the contrary, evidence indicates that humans are born sexually neutral, or Kinsey 3, and have the potential to develop in either or both directions between heterosexuality and homosexuality. According to Ford and Beach (1951), the more sexually repressive societies tend to promote the extremes of 0 or 6; the less repressive societies accept 2, 3, or 4 as the norm. As yet we know very little about the relative degree to which genes, hormones, life experiences, education, or religion push persons in one direction or the other.

Another researcher, Fritz Klein (1993), deepened Kinsey's concepts further. He identifies issues of sexual attraction, sexual behavior, sexual fantasies, emotional preference, social preference, lifestyle, and self-identification, using the Kinsey Rating Scale to obtain a profile from which to construct a multi-dimensional grid. This grid has been helpful in working with persons confused about their sexual orientation. For example, in therapy with a married couple I worked with, the wife wondered whether her husband was gay because he went out for a beer every night after work with the "guys," watched sports every weekend with the "guys," and preferred going out with "guys" socially. While he enjoyed doing things with the family, he had little interest in participating in outings with other couples. In filling out a profile for couples with marital difficulties, I found in this case the husband was a Kinsey 1 on sexual attraction; a 0 on sexual behavior; a 2 on sexual fantasies, a 5 on emotional preference; a 6 on social preference; a 0 on lifestyle; and a 0 on self-identification. In other words, he identified as exclusively heterosexual in sexual behavior, lifestyle, and no experience sexually with men. He had occasional fantasies with men, but basically his fantasy life was heterosexual. On the other hand, he was emotionally and socially comfortable and preferred to be with other men. It was helpful to the couple to get this feedback in negotiating their marriage relationship.

In my experience as a pastor, sex educator and sex therapist, I have not been fully satisfied by either the Kinsey or Klein models. I believe sexual orientation is an even more complex issue, in that I find that people are sexually aroused by more than other people of the same or opposite sex Thus, my definition of sexual orientation is whatever it is that causes a person to have an erotic or romantic response that goes beyond other people of the same gender, other gender or both genders. The thesis of my model is that potentially anything in the universe can have erotic value for someone. Sometimes this can be appropriate, at other times, inappropriate. For example, one can be turned on erotically by the beauty of nature, music, a delicious meal, a favorite scent, a movie, particular clothing, or being tied up or spanked. As I listen to others, I am convinced that there is nothing in this universe that is not an erotic turn-on for someone. However, morally, there are limits: being turned on by hurting oneself, someone else, or acting out sexually with children or a young adolescent is totally inappropriate.

As a sexologist, I am interested in all the dimensions of a person's relationships, sexual and non-sexual, whether with the self, the things in their lives, or with whatever is ultimate in their life. It is my premise that besides responding erotically to another person or persons, people can also find sexual pleasure in relating in all the dimensions of their relationships: self, things (both animate and inanimate), and to whatever the Thou or ultimate reality is in their life. This theory challenges all of the usual theories regarding sexual orientation. In my theory, anything that turns a person on can be described as part of their sexual orientation. I also believe that there can be a spiritual dimension to all these relationships. Martin Buber, the Jewish theologian, in his *I and Thou* was instrumental in the development of my theory.

STAYTON'S PANEROTIC POTENTIAL MODEL

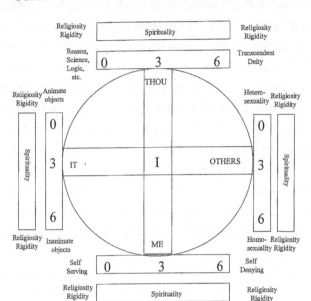

William Stayton has suggested a model of sexual orientation that broadens the focus of the Kinsey Sexual Orientation Scale and Fred Klein's Sexual Orientation Grid, by acknowledging the possibility that individuals can find erotic nurturance and intimacy in almost anything in the universe.

Fig. 2 Stayton's Panerotic Potential Model

Regarding one's relationship with themselves, we know a person can make love to their own body through masturbation, their own genital and body odors, anal stimulation, sex toys, self-pleasuring, self-massage, and other auto-erotic activities. In working with an individual, it is very important to assess the relationship with self. If we introduce a Kinsey-type scale, we would find at one end of the continuum a person who is totally self-absorbed. Pathologically, we call this narcissism. At the other end of the continuum is a person who would deny themself any self-pleasuring. We would diagnose this person as having a martyr-complex syndrome. The ideal of health would be someone in the 3 range, who holds in creative tension the ability both to serve oneself or deny oneself when either would be appropriate, and this would also be true sexually. Self-pleasuring in the context of a healthy self-image can be very helpful in developing one's sexual and erotic response cycle. An almost unanimous perspective in the field of sexuality today is that autoeroticism is healthy, desirable and important to adult sexual adjustment. Masturbation is a lifelong and enjoyable practice for many people. In cases of dysfunction, it is common to recommend masturbation as a part of the treatment plan (if it is within the person's value system). Does this not have implications for contemporary religious education?

Young people should be given an understanding of masturbation and its health-giving benefits throughout the life cycle. We emphasize the importance of healthy self-esteem, yet, almost all religious sexuality education curriculum either presents masturbation as negative or ignores it as if it does not exist. Religious institutions, too often, instill guilt rather than affirmation for this practice, thus causing one to be cut off from an important part of the relationship to the self.

A friend of mine, Dr. Joycelyn Elders, was the 15th Surgeon General of the U.S. from 1993 to 1994 under President Bill Clinton. She was the second woman, second person of color, and the first African American to serve as Surgeon General. She was trained to be a pediatrician. In speaking out at a United Nations conference on AIDS, she frankly expressed her views on controversial issues, such as teaching youth about masturbation. Because of her controversial views, President Clinton fired her as Surgeon General.

Since that time, Dr. Elders returned to her professorship at the University of Arkansas, and also became a member of the adjunct faculty and Advisory Board in the Program in Human Sexuality at the University of Minnesota (UMN). The UMN established the nation's first Joycelyn Elders Chair in Sexual Health Education. The University of Arkansas has also developed a Chair in her name at their school.

Another dimension of a person's relationship is to objects that I call the "Its" continuum. Again, if we introduce a Kinsey-type scale, we would find at one end of the continuum inanimate objects, and at the other end, the animate world. In relation to inanimate objects, erotic responses and sexual pleasure occur with almost any object. I have met people where clothes, art, rubber, leather, vehicles of transportation, nature, explicit erotic material, various scents, money, and parts of the body elicit erotic and sexual responses. This list can be supplemented with literally thousands of other possibilities.

Many years ago, I was invited to speak at a Planned Parenthood affiliate several states away. I was asked if it was okay with me to stay in a private home, rather than a motel. Without hesitating I said "Sure." They housed me with a clergy family. During dinner, the first night, we were sitting at the table: the husband, the wife, their teenaged daughter, and me. I was innocently eating my dinner, when the daughter suddenly said to me: "Have you seen my father's rubber room?" I wasn't sure I heard her correctly. She repeated "Have you seen my father's rubber room yet?" Then she got up from the table and brought back a magazine on "Rubber Fetishism." Her father and mother continued eating their dinner without any reaction. I even wondered if they were hard of hearing. However, after dinner, the family took me upstairs to a room filled with rubber artifacts, and her father told me stories of how he was erotically aroused by all of them. There were rubber artifacts, such as raincoats, fire fighter's gear, rubber tires, sheets, etc. I could not get over the fact that his wife and daughter were there. He had normalized his rubber interest with his family—and me. Since then, I have met others like that minister, although they were not so open with their families.

An interesting follow-up to this story is that 10 years after the experience, I was speaking to the medical and nursing students at the University of Medicine and Dentistry of New Jersey and, in explaining my model to them, I used the experience with the minister and his family as an illustration. Unbeknownst to me, the speaker who was to follow me was the same minister there to speak to the medical and nursing students about "rubber fetishism." He had even brought many rubber artifacts with him to show the students. He told them, much to my relief, that he was the minister of the story I had told them. He said he was pleased that I had, unknowingly, introduced him and he could not wait to tell his wife and their married daughter that I had given this illustration to the students. He affirmed to the audience that my account was correct.

At the other end of the "It" continuum are those who find they are aroused erotically by animate objects, such as a favorite pet or a particular type of animal. It is a fact that many people, especially in our culture, get their touching needs met through their household pets. While this does not usually lead to sexually acting out, the pet can still become the object of the person's preference for an emotional outlet. The vast majority of these experiences do not result in child, adolescent or adult pathology unless the person is discovered in the act of having sex with the animal and made to feel shame or alienation from family or friends. It is in the process of being discovered and the reaction of the discoverer that psychological damage can occur. Of course if animals are the only recipients of a person's sexual feelings, then it is appropriate to refer that person for therapy.

In my university classes on this topic, I would ask the students to write down in three minutes everything they found erotically stimulating. I would tell them not to put their name on the paper. The students would list from 30 items to 60 or more in the three minutes. Examples of what they found sexually arousing are different clothes, art, music, particular foods or drink, settings such as the seashore, a stream, a mountain lake, vacations, or strenuous activities like sports, particular parts of the body, and certain smells. Good communication was also listed as important to a person's ability to experience erotic feelings. I consider these healthy and positive aspects of a person's ability to experience erotic feelings. There were also the unusual, but harmless, objects or activities, such as rubber artifacts, dressing in clothes of the opposite sex, or particular articles of clothing which are needed for erotic arousal. Finally, there were the unusual, but potentially harmful 'turn-ons,' such as being aroused by weapons, infliction of pain or inappropriate acting out sexually that is against public morality. At the end of the semester, I would turn the lights low and ask a student with a sexy voice to read harmless items with love music in the background. It was always a very sensual experience for the class to end on.

Probably the most controversial dimension in my model is the one in relationship to the Thou in one's life, the transcendent dimension, which may or may not include a deity. At one end of the Kinsey scale there are people who do not believe in a deity. The Thou for them might be science, astronomy, logic, or math. After I had offered this theory to a group at an international conference, a participant came up to me and told me he was an astronomer and had an observatory on the top floor of his home. He said he was an atheist. However, a favorite activity of his was to go up to his observatory, point his telescope at a particular part of the universe that he was studying at that time, and get so aroused, he would masturbate.

At the other end of the Thou continuum might be a totally transcendent deity, not related to this life or the earth, totally other-worldly. A healthy response, in my opinion, is a Kinsey 3, that holds in creative balance science and logic with a belief in the transcendent spiritual.

In the years that I have been presenting this model, I have talked with scores of deeply spiritual persons who have experienced sexual pleasure during periods of meditation, prayer and communion. For example, a nun once told me that during a spiritual retreat of 30 days, the first seven days were to be in silent meditation and prayer. After about three days, while in deep meditation, she suddenly had an orgasm and she wasn't even touching herself. While this may sound blasphemous or pathological to some, it seems to make perfect sense to others who have experienced the sensuality and arousal of spiritual feelings. Indeed, the Bible frequently pictures a person's relationship to God with the language of romantic love and marriage. The Bible talks about the bride and bridegroom, the marriage of God and Israel, of Christ and the Church, and of oneness with Christ, so that it does not seem out of context to see a whole relationship with a Creator God as having an erotic component. I have met many clergy who speak of having an erotic response during meaningful worship, meditation, or prayer.

As a young person, one of my favorite events was the occasional Sunday night 'Singspiration' at our church. Some of the gospel tunes that we sang were very sensual indeed. I especially remember "I Come to the Garden Alone"

> I come to the garden alone,
> while the dew is still on the roses.
> And the voice I hear calling in my ear
> the Son of God discloses.
> And He walks with me and He talks with me,
> And He tells me I am his own;
> And the joy we share as we tarry there,
> None other has ever known.

What sensual feelings that hymn used to evoke in me as a teenager. One of my favorite Bible books was the *Song of Songs* (Solomon) with its many erotic passages. It was not unusual for me to read this book, with a flashlight, under the covers at night.

As Bob Francoeur (1991), in his textbook *Becoming a Sexual Person*, discussed Stayton's Panerotic Theory:

> A few artists and poets, like the Pre-Raphaelite Dante Gabriel Rossetti (1828-1882) and the Romantic William Blake (1757-1827), England's greatest visionary poet, have captured the transcendental dimension, human sensuality, and eroticism. The mystical writings of two medieval Spanish saints,

Teresa of Avila and John of the Cross, contain many examples of transcendental erotic expressions in poetry and meditations. In more recent times, the work of anthropologist Loren Eiseley and the astronomer-poet Carl Sagan have touched on the domain of transcendental cosmic sensuality. The Tantric Buddhist tradition of sexuality with its symbolic lingam/yoni (the male and female principles) and the temple sculpture of Hinduism express the transcendental/erotic dimension of Eastern cultures (pg. 522).

As the reader can see, we can be sexual and erotic in all the dimensions of a person's relationships. Therefore, as in the diagram, spirituality can be experienced in each dimension whether with another person of either gender, with oneself, with both animate and inanimate objects, and even with whatever the Thou is in one's life, whether science or a transcendent deity. At the end of each of the Spirituality continua, I have put the descriptive words, "religiosity and rigidity." While this may be debated by some, I do find that when one is locked into the ends of any of the continua, it can lead one to rigidity in "religious" belief systems. I also believe that when one is near the middle of the Kinsey scale on any of the dimensions of relationships, they are often more relaxed, balanced and flexible in their acceptance of both ends of each continuum and a spiritual connection to each.

If nature creates persons who are fully sexual in every sense of the word and in every dimension of their relationships, the question arises as to how we present this erotic aspect in our daily living lifestyle. As we turn to the lifestyles that people choose in their daily living, I think it is also important to see how persons lived out their lives in biblical times. This can be helpful in building a theological framework that is relevant for today. Are there relationships that are both pleasurable and appropriate and relationships which are not? This is the sexuality challenge to religions today.

Chapter 6

LIFESTYLE OPTIONS

FORTY YEARS AGO I WAS INVITED TO GIVE A MAJOR PRE-sentation at an international family life conference in Canada. I was given the topic for my lecture: "Alternative Lifestyles: Marital Options." Even with my training as a clergyman, psychologist, and marriage and family therapist, I knew nothing about this topic. I had been taught there were two healthy lifestyles: monogamous marriage and celibacy if single. If one were single, it would be healthiest to be a priest or nun. Anything other than marriage or a religious vocation was considered as going against home, family, and religious and national heritage. In those days, if you never married, you could expect to be pitied. When I was in grammar school, my parents had a single woman accountant whom they dearly loved. Several times I heard them lament that poor Sophie never found the right man to marry. Actually I learned many years later that Sophie was a lesbian in our church who never came out of the closet to anyone. When I started researching the topic, I soon learned that we live in a different world.

Our children, and indeed we ourselves, have many lifestyle choices, any one of which is considered legitimate by some section of our society. It is a fact that in this 21st century a large proportion of Americans are feeling free to choose from a wide variety of lifestyles. Lifestyle, for the purpose of this chapter, refers to the relational patterns around which individuals organize for daily living. These lifestyles can be heterosexually, homosexually, bisexually, or auto-sexually oriented. Many contemporary women, men, gay persons, young people, married couples, single adults, and older people are pioneers with living in nontraditional ways.

Unfortunately, many clinicians and most clergy are not trained to work with persons living in alternative family lifestyles. Most training in marital and family therapy is based upon a traditional monogamous nuclear lifestyle. It is the experience of many, if not most clinicians that the traditional monogamous marriage is now a minority lifestyle, even within our religious institutions. But what about other marital and family styles? In this chapter, we will explore the concepts behind many of these choices, as well as the types of lifestyles that Americans are choosing today.

Monogamy

Prior to the 16th century, most Western philosophical and religious thinkers were not interested in lifestyle choices, especially within marriage. It is important to distinguish between monogamy (married to one person) and sexual exclusivity (being sexual with that married partner only). Practically all cultures have had alternatives to sexually exclusive monogamy, which were usually reserved for the elite or upper-class citizens. Sexually exclusive monogamy was usually prescribed for the lower and slave classes as a way of controlling them. It may be that sexually exclusive monogamy is not biologically natural for all people, which could account for the fact that so many people are not sexually exclusive. The perception of many people today is that monogamy equals sexual exclusivity. My purpose is not to challenge this view of monogamy nor make a value judgment regarding it, but rather to point out that for many people in our society, monogamy is not an important issue. Certainly, our divorce statistics today indicate commitment to marriage as an institution but not to 'lifelong' monogamy that is sexually exclusive.

Most couples marry with the expectation and hope that each will be able to meet the other's needs as a partner, friend, and lover. Each goes into marriage wanting and making a commitment to fidelity. Since the terms fidelity and infidelity can be defined in many ways and can include many facets of a relationship other than sexual, for our purposes we will limit this discussion to sexual fidelity and infidelity, and we will assume that maintaining a healthy sexual relationship is a primary concern to most couples entering marriage.

It is likely that many who make the commitment to sexual fidelity will not adhere to that commitment throughout their marriage. Couples react differently to changes in commitment; thus, it becomes important to define when a couple is involved in sexual infidelity.

First, there are couples who for various reasons change their commitment to sexual fidelity. They may decide that they want a sexually "open marriage," that is, to include other sexual partners. Thus, their commitment changes so that when one or both spouses become involved sexually with another person, they are not involved in sexual infidelity because they are not violating a commitment to each other. New agreements have been made before new behaviors began.

Second, there are couples who make allowances for certain types of sexual expression outside of marriage. For example, one spouse may want his or her partner to remain sexually exclusive while at home, but will make allowances for the partner to experiment sexually while at a conference or business meeting away from home. Or one or both partners may want certain agreements such as "just don't tell me about it." As long as the partners hold to that agreement, it cannot be said that the couple is engaging in infidelity (even if they have "one-night stands" while away from home) because they are being faithful to their mutually agreed upon commitment.

Third, there are couples who through the years place a high value on sexual exclusivity and who do not want or intend to break their commitment of sexual fidelity. Many couples have the expectation when they marry that they will always completely satisfy one another's needs and will never be attracted to any other person. However, sexual attraction to other persons probably occurs no matter how much in love one is with one's spouse. If couples believe that sexual attraction is akin to sexual infidelity, then just the feeling of attraction can be a real threat to the marriage even though neither acts upon the feeling.

Persons and relationships inevitably change. Thus, it is important for couples to understand that their relationship will most likely change over time. The most critical changes occur in a couple's communication patterns, their sexual relationship, and feelings of closeness and intimacy with one another.

Lifestyle Options

When considering the types of lifestyles people are choosing today, I identified many from my own pastorate, from my students and clients over the years, although there probably is no consensus on the total number and variation. I am listing only those I am familiar with.

Traditional monogamy. It is interesting that this traditional and socially upheld lifestyle is no longer the strongly predominant lifestyle in American culture. In fact, according to Pew Research (pewresearch.org), even the traditional first marriage family, composed of father, mother, and children, accounts for only 46% of all households. Waiting Till Marriage.org claim that about 3% of Americans successfully wait until marriage to have sex, that is,1 in 30 couples, or 10,000,000 people. According to Gallup (news.gallop.com, 5/22/18), about 4.5% of the U.S. population claim to be gay, lesbian, bisexual, or transgender. We do not have a statistic on how many are sexually abstinent until marriage or are a part of the 1 in 30 couples. Regarding divorce rate, the American Psychological Association (APA.org) claims that 50% of first marriages end in divorce, and the divorce rate is even higher in subsequent marriages.

Most couples who marry do so believing that they will be faithfully married "until death do us part." The most serious threat to this lifestyle is not from without but from within, given the high rate of divorce and separation and the number of couples who turn to an alternative lifestyle later in marriage. The APA cites infidelity named in 20 - 40% of divorces (APA.org, 11/12/12). But certainly we should not consider traditional monogamy on its way out as a viable lifestyle, as there are many who will continue to choose this pattern as a fulfilling and valued way of life.

We cannot conclude that sexual fidelity is the only healthy, correct marital lifestyle or conversely, that sexual fidelity is an unhealthy marital lifestyle. Other criterion for accepting extramarital relationships might include such factors as a couple who do not experience jealousy or sense of genital possessiveness, and at the same time have a good and meaningful sexual relationship with each other. The illness of one partner might preclude a meaningful sexual relationship, as may be true of mental illness or coma, so that extra-marital sex might be understood and condoned.

Arranged marriage. This is a marriage that is usually planned by the family, typically by the parents of the couple. According to several resources arranged marriages occur in well over 50% of marriages world-wide today (https://brandongaille.com/25-shocking-arranged-marriages-statistics, 5/20/17; https://brides.com/story/modern-arranged-marriages, 8/27/20). In India today, it is estimated that 90% of marriages are still arranged. For many, however, the couple have more freedom to decline the family's choice. Hinduism is the most widely followed religion in India. When my spouse and I were in India in 2007, we had the opportunity to view a wedding ceremony of two families joining together with the bride and groom representing their families. We visited or stayed in the home of several couples in an arranged marriage where both families were involved in bringing the bride and groom together. In one, the bride and groom represented the joining of the two families. In this family all the married children stayed with the husbands' parents. With the couple we were visiting, there was little communication between the couple or between the wife and her husband's family with whom they were living. They were open that theirs was not a happy marriage. We also stayed with a family where the parents were in an arranged marriage. They told us that over the years they developed a deep love for each other and their children. We visited with a family where the father left the home when the children were young because he did not love the wife his parents had chosen for him. She reared their daughters alone.

Besides India, other countries where arranged marriage is prominent are China, Pakistan, Japan, Israel, Afghanistan, Iran, Iraq and Indonesia. Islamic law and the Muslim religion believe in arranged marriage but having the consent of both parties is preferred. Iran and Iraq are good examples. Indonesia and China are strongly influenced by Buddhist religion. These countries are also advocates of arranged marriages.

In Judaism, it is not uncommon for many Orthodox and Jewish fundamentalists to advocate for arranged marriage. While Christianity does not advocate arranged marriage, it is not unusual for some Christian communities to advocate marrying a person who is in the same faith.

Child-free relationships. It is very difficult for most people who have children to understand those who decide against parenthood. While infertility may preclude giving birth for some, there are a growing number of couples today who want to be in a long-term relationship but who feel that their lives will be more meaningfully fulfilled if they remain childless. Not many years ago, this decision would have been unthinkable. It was traditional that couples who did not have children were to be pitied and were encouraged to adopt so that their "marriage could be complete." Marriage and parenthood have often been thought of as synonymous in our culture. But those who choose a child-free lifestyle today are making the choice for valid and justifiable reasons. With the growing world population and climate change, environmental devastation, and nuclear warfare as real threats, couples may not feel as guilty for not procreating, although the pressure may still be there. Other, more personal factors that can affect this decision are dual careers, the influence of divorce from the couple's own childhood, interracial and interfaith considerations, or physical inability to conceive.

Single parenthood. There are a good number of responsible members of our community today who are saying that, although they do not want to be bound in a permanent relationship, they do want the benefits of parenthood. Both women and men are choosing to rear a child or children without a partner in marriage. It is also true that single parenthood is a transitional lifestyle for many persons such as divorced persons. Many hope that they will remarry at some point in their future.

Today about one-fourth of U.S. children are living with an unmarried parent (FactTank, pewresearch.org, 12/12/19). A lot of single parents did not choose to be single parents. Many of them have left their relationship to rear children alone. No definite statistics on the number of never-married men choosing single parenthood are available. However, it is not unusual to find ads in the personal columns of magazines or online sources through which a man is seeking a woman to bear his child. I know quite a few single gay men who are choosing to adopt a child.

Many fertility clinics have made their services available to single women who are seeking artificial insemination, a procedure that is safe and involves few legal complications. Some singles use terms like "elective parent" and "single parent by choice" to describe their lifestyle.

I had a single man who came to me because I taught in a university human sexuality doctoral program. He said that he was not married and did not see marriage in his future. He did, however, want to be a father. His question was whether one of our female students would be open to having a child by him. He said he would donate his sperm to a sperm bank for her to be inseminated. He was wealthy and offered to pay her total tuition, room and board, and $200 a month for her years at the university. After the birth of the child, he would also give her an additional $50,000 a year for 5 years. What an offer for a graduate student! I asked him what if the child was born with a disability or multiple disabilities? His answer was that he would pay for the care of that child for life because it was his child. Though sympathetic with his desire to become a father, I told him that I could not act on his request because it would be unethical, if not illegal, and would cost me my job. I suggested that he consult a lawyer.

The fact that up to 34 percent of our school children come from couples who are divorced and live with one parent has contributed to removing the stigma of illegitimacy once associated with out-of-wedlock births (kidscount.org).

Singlehood. According to the U.S. Census Bureau, (2/11/2020), over 45% of the adult population in the U.S.,18 and older, were divorced, widowed or have always been single. This is the largest number of single adults ever in the U.S. Marriage is not something many of these single persons permanently avoid, but is rather a state they choose not to enter for the time being for many valid reasons, such as career choices or not having found a partner they wanted to marry. While it is true that many of these persons will later marry, there is a definite trend toward staying single longer. The average age of first marriage currently (Census.gov, 2019), for women was almost 28 and for men over 29. As was not true in earlier generations, persons who do not marry are thankfully not considered second-class citizens.

Cohabitation. In this lifestyle two or more people live together in a relationship that is similar to marriage but lacks the legal ties. According to Pew Research Center (11/6/2019), marriage rates have gone down steadily since 2000, while the rate of cohabitation has gone up dramatically. By 2019, the number of cohabiting couples had risen 138% since 1990 and 29% from 2007 alone. Forty percent of unmarried households have children.

In the past, legal marriage was not an option for LGBT couples. However, two years after the 2015 Supreme Court decision that LGBT could marry Gallup reports that 10.2% had entered such a union. As a pastor and in a church, one marriage ceremony I conducted was between a Protestant clergy transman and a former Roman Catholic nun. They met in a chaplaincy training program and fell in love. He became a hospital chaplain.

For some young adults, according to the U.S. Census Bureau, living together has become a more common option than marriage.

It is not unusual to find parents who encourage their adult children to live together with a prospective marriage partner for awhile before getting married. A reason often given is that marriage is meant to last for a long time and these parents want their children to be absolutely sure of the decision they are making. There are parents who do not want their children to repeat their own mistakes by entering into a marriage that doesn't work out or getting married for the wrong reasons, and they believe cohabitation may be helpful.

Another phenomenon is the increasing number of persons who are cohabiting before entering into a second (or later) marriage. A reason often given is that they want the choice to be right and responsible. Nevertheless, 67% of second marriages and 73% of third marriages end in divorce! (APA.org)

More and more couples in their middle and later years are now choosing cohabitation. The number of couples over 50 who entered into a cohabitation lifestyle increased 75% from 2007 to 2016, the highest increase in any age group, according to Pew. A former editor of *The Journal of Marriage and Family* wrote "Americans are far more accepting now…and the people turning 60 are very different from the people who were 60 twenty years ago." It is true that most laws regarding marriage are for the protection of children. Cohabitation offers companionship, wider social circles, and sexual intimacy at an age when the same persons would otherwise face isolation. It can also provide better economic stability as well as economic protection. As an example, many older adults have debts, mortgages, and college loans to pay off that are not part of a cohabiting partner's debt. Being married can also affect government and pension benefits. Many find cohabitation avoids inheritance problems for the children.

Serial monogamy. Most people who become divorced may want to remarry, and many do. The trend, however, is that fewer remarry, and those who do take longer to make that decision. The majority, both married and unmarried, of those who go from one monogamous relationship to another are, however, looking for one that is more mature and fulfilling than the previous one. While married or unmarried, these persons are monogamous, and during their adult lives they may be involved in a number of such relationships, thus, the term serial monogamy. As mentioned previously a sizable number in this group will live together before remarriage.

Communes. In the past, communal living was seen more as an option for young unmarried adults starting their life at college or in business. However, in times of ecological and economic crises, communal living can also be an attractive option. In the 1970s and 1980s, thousands of communes developed across the country. They were found at every level of society, both economic and educational. People live together for many and varied reasons: professional, philosophical, political, therapeutic, religious, economic, or some combination of these. Participants can be single, married, divorced, or widowed. At those times, many people, in order to maintain the economic style of living to which they were accustomed, found a solution in communal living.

In the 1970s, during an economic downturn, a group of American Baptists, with encouragement from their denomination, lived communally near Philadelphia in a Roman Catholic abbey which was no longer in use. As a consultant to this group I felt involved in the life of this community. There were eight family units, from a one-person unit to married couples without children to married couples with children. The age range of the group was from three to mid-50s. The community was interested in ecology, as well as in building relational support systems among its members. They found that among them they had 12 automobiles but needed only eight. Instead of eight refrigerators, washers, dryers, and other appliances, they needed less than half that number when they were living communally. They shared household chores, which meant that each had less work than in their single-unit houses. Each family unit had its own private space as well as community space: a common kitchen, dining room, living room, playroom, and library. They had one meal a day together, usually dinner; the other meals were fixed individually. The community remained together until the Catholic order took the abbey over again. All the members felt that the five-year experience had been a very valuable and significant part of their lives and, although the majority returned to their single-unit lifestyle, many of them said they would live communally again under the right circumstances.

Swinging and/or group sex. Most men and women have probably fantasized about a sexual relationship with someone other than their current partner or spouse. Today a growing number of couples are making this fantasy a reality. According to the *Journal of Human Sexuality* (2019), there are approximately 13 million people in the United States engaged in the swinging lifestyle. It is said that besides being racially diverse, "these people tend to be more conservative, more religious, more honest, more open-minded, more educated, more professional, and better off financially than the average American." Most often these people lead conventional lives in every other respect.

Swingers are couples who meet other couples with the intention of pairing off for sexual and/or sensual experiences with someone new. Individuals and couples who do not belong to an organized swingers' group may join together as friends for sexual purposes. They consider sex a healthy, recreational pastime rather than as a sin, vice, or indulgence in perversion. Contrary to popular myths, some research studies have found that swingers often rate their marriages as happier and more fulfilling than do those couples who have no other intimate relationships. I have known several swinger couples, none of whom fit our society's stereotyped "far out" picture of such people, including a 75-year-old couple who have been married for over 45 years.

While this sexual lifestyle may meet with disapproval in the population at large and in most religious communities, it is important to remember that this is a mutually agreed upon lifestyle between the partners and it does receive support from other swingers. Swingers then have the advantage of an internalized ideology that considers their behavior both moral and desirable. The swinger couples with whom I have talked insist that they strongly value fidelity in their marriages, but they discuss fidelity in terms of an open, honest, and trusting relationship.

There seem to be at least three types of swingers: those who desire only sex with an outside partner, without social or emotional expectations; the recreational swingers who see the social aspects of swinging as being as important as the sexual aspects and who often belong to private clubs with rather stable memberships; and finally, those who are seeking close and lasting relationships with their outside partners. Out in the country, near where I presently live, is a large building with a big sign and under the name, it says "A Private Club." Every weekend there are many cars in its parking lot. It is listed in the State Swinger's Guide.

Polyamory/group marriage. While monogamy is the only legally accepted marriage, there are those in our society who are choosing to live in a marriage-type relationship involving three or more committed adults. Some polyamorous or group marriages are closed, in that sexual intimacy is kept within the bounds of the relationship. Others have an agreement that allows members of the marriage to have other outside sexual contacts. My first experience with group marriage clients—two men and one woman who came to my office—was very helpful to my understanding of some of the dynamics and pressures involved in this lifestyle. The woman and one of the men, legally married, met and subsequently became close friends with the second man—close on almost every level: intellectual, emotional, social, and spiritual. As they described it, "it was a logical and smooth transition for our feelings of intimacy to be expressed on a physical/sexual level." They had their three-person union solemnized by a member of the clergy. Their purchase of a home together precipitated the twofold problem that they brought to me. First, because of their lifestyle, the neighbors had signed a petition against their living in that neighborhood. Second, one of the men was in danger of losing his job because his employer felt that his lifestyle was offensive to his religion and to the public they served. The threesome wanted my help in learning how to build a greater understanding between themselves and those who were against them. They were very sincere about wanting to be creative in educating their critics. In the end they sold their home and bought in a more friendly and accepting community, joined an accepting church community, and the one man changed his job when his employer refused to discuss the matter further.

As we worked together on their problem, I developed a real appreciation of their love and commitment to one another. They had no other outside sexual relationships but were committed to the idea of fidelity in their marriage.

Open-ended relationship in marriage. Some couples, although they want to be married, just cannot be happy with a closed monogamous relationship. If both partners agree they may decide to enter into an open-ended marriage. In this arrangement both are free to establish other independent, significant relationships. Sexual exclusiveness may or may not be part of the open contract. Open-ended marriage can be growth-producing and successful for some couples, especially if they already have a strong and rewarding sexual and emotional relationship with one another. However, I have never known an open relationship to save a troubled marriage. This lifestyle has no place in a relationship that is characterized by jealousy and possessiveness.

I met an older couple at one of my workshops on Relationships and Sexuality who had been married for more than 40 years. The wife was diagnosed as having multiple sclerosis (MS) shortly after their marriage. In obtaining information on the disease the couple discovered that sexual apathy would be a symptom as the illness progressed. They discussed this in depth over many months, and even though they were very religious, they decided that a way they could combat the apathy and its effect on their relationship would be to open their marriage to include other sexual partners. For over 35 years they had an open marriage and each had a number of significant sex partners, while maintaining their own sexual relationship. Interestingly, the wife was free of MS symptoms for that same amount of time. They both attribute her symptom-free years, their good sex life, and their strong marriage to the openness they shared. Becoming active in a progressive church tradition helped them to work through their own values regarding their lifestyle choice. Forty years ago their pastor helped them to look at their motives and the consequences of their choices and to develop criteria for making their decisions based on what would build love and trust, enhance communication, and encourage cooperation and mutuality. After weighing all the above factors they chose an open marriage.

The well-respected couples' therapist Esther Perel, in her book *The State of Affairs: Rethinking Infidelity* (2017) gives extensive data on extramarital relations. She identifies different personality and marital types and based on given combinations, is able to help particular couples to have a successful, open marriage contract. According to the *Journal of Sex and Marital Therapy* (4/20/2016) one in five single people have experimented with some form of an open relationship with a couple.

There is growing acceptance of ethical non-monogamy as a practice for people, especially in the queer community, who are in committed relationships. A helpful discussion of this issue is found in a podcast by Peter McGraw (2017) on "What is Ethical Monogamy." This could be a very helpful discussion for a religious community to have.

Synergamous relationship. I first read about this lifestyle concept in the book *Thursday, My Love* (Rimmer, 1972). The idea is that a couple involved in a primary relationship go on to develop a committed secondary relationship. The resulting secondary couple may even set up another residence where they spend time, which could be one day a week (as in *Thursday, My Love*), or one weekend a month, or one month a year. Ideally, the primary partner knows about and approves of the secondary relationship. While some may label this marriage "bigamy," I have met several couples who have a synergamous marriage and it seems to have a different and very meaningful quality. I have also known several couples where one or both partners are bisexual. These people have found a synergamous relationship to be ideal for their marriage, since it allows the bisexual partner an opportunity to have a committed same-sex arrangement. In two of the situations the secondary relationship of one of the partners has been ongoing for several years and in each case the spouse knows and approves.

Family network system. In this lifestyle, also known as the voluntary extended family, two or more family units join together as a way of sharing life's experiences (e.g., meals, vacations, special events) and as an emotional support system. In a world too often filled with loneliness and isolation, the family network system can fill a real need. Sharing sexual intimacy with other members of the network may or may not be part of the system.

It seems to me that fulfilling a supportive role was an original intention, sociologically, of our religious institutions. At times the church, mosque, or synagogue has been, and for many still is, the center of family life. It provided a support system for family members and was the center of social, cultural, educational, and recreational activities for the family. Today, in our highly mobile and compartmentalized culture, the religious institutions have too often lost the feeling of the family network system. Thus, many families are reaching out on their own to establish and become a part of an expanded network that will help them to feel less isolated and alienated from others.

If I am to describe my own family lifestyle it would fit best under this category for at least a few years. My spouse and I moved to the East Coast from the West Coast and also started a family. Following my graduate work, I took a couple of positions, finally ending up with a professorship at the University of Pennsylvania. We had four children and no primary family for 3,000 miles. Through our church, we joined with two other families, both of whom, like ourselves had no relatives in the area. For a couple years, we established a family network system by having three evening meals together each week. On a rotating basis the host family prepared the meal and cleaned up afterwards. We also shared tools, helped each other with home repairs or maintenance, and often socialized together. We also, at times, vacationed together, adding other church families. Our particular network pattern did not include sharing sexually intimate relationships. It certainly was a rewarding experience and all of us received valuable support in times of stress and crises. After the children grew up and left, we no longer met, except for special occasions, but kept friendships with each family.

Chaste monogamy. It is difficult to know how many couples are living in a chaste relationship, but from my own clinical practice I know that it does exist. There are couples who have an otherwise excellent relationship but have no sexual desire or activity. A phenomenon often seen by therapists is the Madonna/whore syndrome. In this syndrome women are divided into two types. The Madonna represents the woman who, held up and adored, is the person one marries and cares for but for whom one has no sexual desire or need (other than to have children) and whose model is the Virgin Mary. The other type of woman is the whore, representing the woman of passion and sexual appetite, the woman who is sensual, sexual and seductive. If both partners view the married woman as "Madonna" they are likely to develop a fulfilling chaste marriage after procreational needs are met. If only one partner exemplifies this syndrome, a chaste marriage may exist but without sexual fulfillment for either partner. Negative reasons for a relationship becoming chaste are hostility, boredom, apathy, illness and depression.

Some gay couples may experience this same phenomenon, with high sexual activity at the beginning of their relationship, but as it develops into a deeper love and commitment, believe that their relationship should not be defined by high sexual activity and settle into a chaste relationship. Some are able to settle into this change and some are not and thus end the relationship.

Incestuous relationships and marriage. In the United States today, biological and cultural incest still occurs and the statistics are believed to be underreported. For example, it is well-known that one in four girls and one in five-to-seven boys have been sexually involved with an adult, and an overwhelming number occur within the family. Early in my therapy practice, I had a family where the father had a child with his daughter. The family decided to stay together and the child was reared by the grandmother/mother, the grandfather/father, and mother/half-sister.

All incestual relationships are legal in N.J. as long as it is consensual and between adults over 18 years old. For example, as reported in *New York Magazine*, a father married his daughter and they live legally in New Jersey (thecut. com, 1/15/2015). New York State's highest court blessed a marriage between an uncle and his niece in 2014 (*New York Post*, 10/29/14). Currently, in America, only 24 states prohibit marriage between first cousins. Another seven states allow marriage between cousins under special circumstances. Nineteen states and the District of Columbia allow such marriages between adult cousins. Charles Darwin and Albert Einstein both married first cousins. Franklin D. Roosevelt married his cousin, although Eleanor was not a first cousin. There are many other first cousin marriages among public figures. It is estimated that 250,000 persons are in first cousin marriages in the U.S.; 20 percent of all couples worldwide are first cousins; and, surprisingly, a fairly high percentage of all marriages historically have been between first cousins (Wikipedia). According to Dr. Arno Motulsky in a study reported in the *Journal of Genetic Counseling* (April 2002), there is a low risk, less than 7%, of having a child with birth defects.

Lifelong celibacy and chastity. Some persons choose a lifestyle of lifelong celibacy and chastity. Their reasons may be based on religious vows, as in the case of priests and nuns, or simply on the fact that they have never found a partner with whom they want to develop a sexual relationship.

Other reasons for choosing celibacy and chastity include a fear of sexual intimacy or a lack of need for and/or interest in a sexual relationship. They may define themselves, and are comfortable with, being non-sexual or asexual.

Internet relationships. According to the American Psychological Association (*APA Monitor*, 3/20/2011, "Are Internet affairs different?") there must be a rethinking of infidelity to include chatroom sexual conversations and cybersex. The question is, if there is no physical contact or actual sex, should it still be considered an affair? "While there is no universally accepted definition, an internet affair frequently involves intimate chat sessions and sexually stimulating conversation or cybersex, which may include filming masturbation with a Web camera. Several studies suggest that even when there is no in-person contact, online affairs can be just as devastating as the real-world variety, triggering feelings of insecurity, anger and jealousy...While men traditionally have been the more unfaithful sex, gender roles are reversing in some cases as more women experience cybersex" (*APA Monitor*, 3/20/2011).

The internet has certainly opened new ways of exploring sexuality and infidelity. This exploration also takes place in the home on the computer and even when spouse and children are somewhere else in the same home. Fantasy, self-esteem, and body image can be enhanced by the internet experience. Some even set up a second life with a partner they may never see, through avatars, who build houses together, go on trips, and participate in different activities and events. One husband I saw had a second life with a woman half-way across the world. Through avatars, they built a home, started a successful business, and traveled to exotic places, all on the internet. His wife was intrigued with this activity, until it took up all his time when he was at home and even wanted his dinner brought to him while he was online because his life was so exciting he couldn't eat with his family most nights. Another client, a woman, found she was online so much that it was affecting her marriage and she hoped that therapy would help her quit the activity which she enjoyed more than her everyday life.

The internet has become a real challenge to both adults and youth regarding sexuality. The importance of taking responsibility, improving communication, contextualizing real life from fantasy life, and developing skills to build better real-life relationships is an opportunity and challenge in both education and therapy. It is important to help couples and families to work on issues of trust, betrayal and forgiveness.

The secret affair. Finally, I add to the above list the seemingly monogamous relationship in which one or both of the partners carry on a secret affair. It is difficult to know how many people are having or have had a secret affair. It is believed that more men than women are likely to have a secret affair. Estimates from the research literature range from 13% to 45% for married women and from 20% to 65% of married men engage in extramarital relationships at some time during their marriage. While the majority of these are totally secret and unknown to the partner, others are secret, but their partners may be suspicious that an affair has occurred or is currently happening.

In general secret affairs are not helpful to the primary relationship. The amount of energy used to nourish the relationship and maintain its secrecy can rob the primary relationship of the kind of energy needed to keep it alive and healthy. This type of lifestyle is usually a forced choice and not a person's preferred pattern. Having chosen to participate in an affair, the person would often prefer to be able to be open with their spouse. More often than in other lifestyles discussed, the person involved here is filled with guilt, shame and remorse and is not interested in dissolving the primary relationship. Secret affairs can consist of anything from a one-time experience to an ongoing and committed sexual relationship.

It is important to note, however, that in some cases the extramarital relationship is a possible outlet for a partner who may have a greater sexual need or capacity than their spouse, or in cases where physical disability or illness of one's partner precludes sexual activity. In a situation where the partners' sexual relationship is unsatisfactory, an extramarital affair may give the involved partner important new insights into sexual communication and make an improved primary relationship possible.

As a pastor, educator and therapist, I would not ever advocate the secret affair lifestyle because of the deceptive factor. First of all, many "secret" affairs sooner or later become known. When the information does become known, the spouse often admits that they either knew, suspected, or at least was not surprised. It is very difficult, I believe, to live in an intimate relationship and keep an extramarital relationship a secret unless the communication between partners has totally broken down and they are virtually living separate lives anyway. Second, it is very difficult, if not impossible, to help a couple strengthen and grow in their relationship while one partner is maintaining an outside affair. Since many of the couples I have seen were involved in a secret affair, one of the primary goals of therapy was to resolve how the issue of that affair would be dealt with in the context of marital therapy. I believe if the affair is to remain a secret, then the goals of increased intimacy and communication will be compromised. As a therapist, I then had to decide in each case whether I would be able to work with that particular client.

Conclusion: Alternative Lifestyles: Right or Wrong?

There will no doubt be those who read this chapter and immediately come to the conclusion that what is being discussed is either sinful or a manifestation of neurotic conflicts regarding intimacy issues and disturbed object relations. They may or may not be correct. There will also be those who read this chapter and proclaim how healthy it is that more and more people are breaking the bonds of traditional lifestyles and developing relational patterns that are more fulfilling to them. This latter group too may or may not be correct. I would make the following observations to my readers.

First, the lifestyles mentioned in this chapter are neither being advocated nor disavowed. They are all lifestyles that are being chosen by large numbers of people. What is being offered is a description of the various lifestyles, some statistics if they are available, and occasional examples from my own experiences as a pastor, educator, and a marital and family therapist.

Second, there is certainly no unanimity among the various professions in religion, education, therapy, or research as to what is or is not a healthy lifestyle. If each lifestyle could be dissected there would still be diverse opinions as to whether it is healthy or not.

Third, there can be healthy or pathological aspects in any of the lifestyles. Although there are no statistics available, there is probably no more pathology, proportionately, among the alternative lifestyles as in the more traditional lifestyle of a heterosexual, monogamous marriage and family. There are moral and socially responsible persons to be found in all of them and, if we were to analyze the lifestyles of people we associate with in our everyday life, we would no doubt discover that many of these individuals have at one time or another, been involved in more than one of these lifestyles. Thus, the lifestyles I have described are not mutually exclusive.

Fourth, after reviewing the various lifestyles I found in my research, we will look at and compare with the alternative lifestyles described in the Bible, which we will learn neither advocated nor disavowed a monogamous marriage!

One final thought. As a society we need to be more accepting of, and open to, the various alternatives that fit people's emotional, social, spiritual, and sexual needs or desires. If these alternatives involve no inherent physical or emotional harm and no infringement on the rights of others, then it is my judgement that a chosen lifestyle has the right to exist—as an individual's "preferred way of life."

Marriage in Biblical Times

Many religious people say to me "if only we could get back to the biblical view of marriage." But what was this biblical point of view? What I found is that scholars have identified many patterns or forms of marriage in the Bible. This comes as a surprise to many people.

Matriarchal marriage. One of the earliest forms of marriage in the Bible is matriarchal, where the children were named after the mother. There were two Biblical forms of matriarchal marriage. The first is "Beena," where the children remain in the home of the mother, as does the husband. He moves in with her. Jacob (Genesis 30) and Moses (Exodus 2) are examples. The second is known as "Mota," where the wife stays with her family and the husband comes to visit her. Samson is a good example of this form of marriage (Judges 14-15).

Patriarchal marriage. This is a common form of marriage in the Bible. In this marriage, descent and authority are reckoned from the father. The father names the child. The essence of the self is seen as transmitted from father to son. The husband has power over his wife. She is part of his property and totally under his control. The Hebrew term "baal" is both "owner of property" and "husband". The verb may mean "to possess" or "to marry." Jeremiah (Jeremiah 18: 18-23) and Paul (Ephesians 5: 22-24) speak to this meaning.

Polygamy. The term polygamy literally means "many marriages" usually existing concurrently in the same family or family group. It actually is the most common form of marriage in the Bible. Abraham (Genesis 15-22), Jacob (Genesis 29-30), and David (I Chronicles 3) are examples of this lifestyle.

Monogamy. While the majority of religious people may believe monogamy is the major lifestyle taught by the Bible, it is interesting to note that it is neither prescribed nor proscribed in the Bible (no references available to support either).

Exogamy. Exogamy is where a marriage takes place outside the defined kinship circle which is defined differently in various parts of the Bible. For example, Esau (Genesis 36) had two Canaanite wives, a Horite wife, and a wife who was one of Ishmael's daughters (Genesis 16). Ishmael was a son of Abraham, whose descendants became Islamic; Joseph (Genesis 41) had an Egyptian wife; and Moses (Exodus 2) was married to an Ethiopian woman. A present day example of exogamy would be a Jewish person marrying an Arab; an Asian marrying a Caucasian; an African marrying a person from India, etc.

Endogamy. Endogamy is where marriage is restricted to members of the group or religion. A biblical example would be not marrying outside the community of Israel. There are numerous present day examples, such as not wanting a son or daughter to marry someone of their own gender, or outside their own religion or race or nation. When we were in France, we met a French couple who were incensed that their son married a woman from Great Britain. They were sure that she would never be able to cook a meal properly or that their children would not learn to speak French correctly.

Levirate marriage. The word "levir" means "a husband's brother." Genesis 38 gives an example of Onan. When his older brother died, he was ordered by his father to impregnate his brother's wife so that his brother's children would get the inheritance due the older son. Instead, Onan pulled out of his sister-in-law before ejaculation so she could not become pregnant. He let his semen fall on the ground. His father had him killed for not fulfilling his duty to his brother. This is a very interesting story worth recounting further. The father's daughter-in-law left and went back to her own family. Later, she learned that her father-in-law was going to be passing through their town and she covered herself like a prostitute and lured him to have sex with her, without knowing who she was. In order to have sex with her, she asked him for a sign of who he was. He gave her his staff, a cord and his ring. She actually became pregnant by him and had twins. She achieved the inheritance. It is interesting how religious teaching has linked this story with masturbation as the sin. Even the dictionary names masturbation and self-gratification as "onanism" when the reality is that Onan was practicing coitus interruptus.

Incestuous Marriage and Relationships. There are at least 14 different stories in the Bible about incest (sex between close kin). The Bible does not differentiate between biological incest where a bloodline is involved, and cultural incest, which includes but goes beyond biological incest. Taboos vary between cultures. Most of biblical stories occurred before the Jewish people migrated from Egypt to Palestine and the giving of the Mosaic anti-incest laws, found in Leviticus 18: 8-18 and 20: 11-21 and in parts of Deuteronomy. Leviticus 18 lists all forbidden sexual relationships, but cousin sexual relationships are not included. It is interesting to note that in ancient times brother-sister, father-daughter, mother-son, cousin-cousin, aunt-nephew, uncle-niece, and other combinations of relations were not unusual. In royal families, for example, men and women were married as a means of perpetuating the royal lineage. Moses was reared in a royal household. Following are other examples of incestuous relationships in the Bible:

1. Noah's son saw his nakedness (Genesis 9:20-27) and according to the Talmud (Sanhedrin 70a) his son may have sodomized his father. Some scholars today have suggested that he may have had intercourse with his father's wife.

2. Abraham's brother, Nahor, married his niece, a daughter of another brother (Genesis 11:29).

3. Lot's two daughters seduced him, were impregnated by him, each had a son, and the half-brothers were both Lot's sons and grandsons (Genesis 19: 32-38).

4. Abraham wife, Sarah, was his half-sister (Genesis 20:12).

5. Abraham's brother, Nahor, married his niece, Milcah (Genesis 24:15).

6. Abraham's son, Issac, married his cousin once removed, Rebekah, the granddaughter of Nahor and Milcah (Genesis 24:15).

7. Isaac and Rebekah's son, Jacob, married his cousins who were sisters, Leah and Rachel, daughters of Rebekah's brother (Genesis 29: 16-30).

8. Jacob's son, Reuben, had sex with his father's concubine, Bilhah (Genesis 35:22).

9. Judah, one of Jacob's sons, mistook Tamar, his daughter-in-law, for a prostitute and impregnated her and she had twins. (Genesis 38). The story of this relationship was discussed under the Levirite marriage above.

10. Anram married his paternal aunt, Jochebed, and they had two sons, Aaron and Moses (Exodus 6:20).

11. King David's son, Amnon, raped his half-sister, Tamar. It is interesting to note that when Amnon was pleading with Tamar to have sex with him, she told him that if he would ask their father, David, that he would give permission, but he didn't and raped her instead (2 Samuel 13: 13-14).

12. Absalom, another son of King David, had sex with his father's wives and concubines (2 Samuel 14:27; 16: 22).

13. Obeying the Lord's command, Zelophehad's five daughters married their cousins (Numbers 36: 1-11).

14. Caleb said, "Whoever strikes Kiriath-sepher and captures it, to him will I gave Achsah my daughter as wife." Othniel was given his cousin, Achsah, as wife (Joshua 15: 16-17).

15. According to the Roman Catholic encyclopedia New Advent (newadvent.org), Religious Forums (religiousforums.com), and The Church of Jesus Christ of Latter Day Saints (lds.org), it is possible that Joseph and Mary, parents of Jesus, were first

cousins as a result of a Levirite marriage (Matthew 1:16, Luke 3:23 NRSV).

The initiation of the marriage contract. In the Bible, usually the father, as head of the family instituted the marriage plans, selected the spouse and planned the marriage party.

Marriage by capture. This may or may not be found in the Bible; however, in Judges, Leviticus, and Deuteronomy there is some indication of this type of marriage. It occurred when females were scarce.

Marriage by purchase. Jacob's marriage to Leah and Rachel are examples of this form of marriage (Genesis 31:15).

Marriage by covenant. Two families enter into a covenant who thereby form an alliance through their representatives, the bridegroom and the bride. Marriage was both personal and communal.

Betrothal. Betrothal, including sexual relationships, seemed to be equivalent to marriage in the Bible. Deuteronomy 20: 6-7, Lot (Genesis 19), Samson (Judges 14-16), and Joseph (Matthew 1:18, 20, 24-25) suggest this concept. Sexually, it was similar to engagement in modern times where the majority of couples have a sexual relationship before the actual marriage ceremony. There were no marriage ceremonies in the Bible. There could be parties and celebrations. For example, in John 2:1-11, Jesus was invited to a wedding in Cana and when the "party" ran out of wine, Jesus turned water into the best wine. This miracle convinced his disciples to believe in him. Marriage simply consisted of a man and woman, with the consent of her father or guardian, living together and beginning a family. There were no vows, no rabbi, no ritual, no prayers, no pronouncement, no license, and no registration.

Final Conclusion

Even in the Bible, as in the United States today, there were lifestyle options that were accepted in different parts of biblical tradition. Again, as diversity is the key to understanding biological and psychological development, so also is diversity important in understanding the different lifestyles that persons have been living throughout history. In summary, there are many models for relationships, both in contemporary life and in biblical times, that are considered acceptable. Just as important is the fact that an act-centered theology has little meaning in contemporary relationships or in biblical relationships. Both relationships in contemporary lifestyle options as well as in biblical times are centered around a relationship-centered theology.

Next, we will turn to the importance of understanding the sexual and erotic response cycles in a person and the impact that religion has often had in being helpful or harmful to one's sexual and erotic response.

Chapter 7

SEXUAL AND EROTIC RESPONSE CYCLES

WE ARE BORN SEXUAL AND EROTICALLY RESPONSIVE. WE are not born "lovers." To be a good lover is a skill we need to learn; it does not come naturally. Most people are ignorant about their sexuality and their sexual and erotic responses because knowledge about sex is too often not valued in our culture. And yet we live in a culture that bombards us with sex in advertising, on the internet, in our movies—but most of it does not help us create healthy sexual self-image and fulfilling sexual experiences. We learn more about sex as sin than as pleasure. As seen in the next section, there is also a socialization process that is not helpful.

Goal-Directed versus Pleasure-Directed Sex

Unfortunately, in American culture, males are too often socialized to be goal-directed in their approach to sex. To the majority of males, the penis is the central focus and everything else, such as sensual touch, is only important when it leads to the goal of intercourse and orgasm. All too often, the ultimate goal is simultaneous orgasm, the big "OO," which rarely happens for most couples. Females are socialized to be more sensual in their approach to sex, and are often brought up to believe their focus is on the sensuality of sex, such as kissing and caressing of their body, and not focused on their genitals. Too many females grow up to believe that their genitals are dirty, ugly, and smelly. Males and females miss each other in this cross-sexualization emphasis. In a healthy relationship, both males and females need to be both sensually and genitally focused whether in a heterosexual or same-sex relationship.

Goal-directed sex is viewed like a series of steps. The first step might be "the look." The next step is the "invitation" to be together. Next is kissing, then maybe the following: fondling, breast stimulation, genital touching, oral sex, intercourse, and all leading to the goal of the big "O" orgasm. After orgasm, it is all over until the next time.

Pleasure-directed sex is like a circle with many spokes, each of which can be an end in itself. The spokes may be kissing, fondling, breast stimulation, genital play, sex toy play, oral sex, vaginal intercourse, and anal sex. Any of these may or may not lead to the big "O." The only goal is what is pleasurable.

Thus, the only goals in a healthy sexual relationship should be based on good and open communication and being pleasure-directed. The foundation of a good sexual relationship is communication. Couples need to be able to talk comfortably with each other about what feels good, what doesn't feel good, what is allowable, what is off-limits, and what either or both partners want to or are willing to try. This is the meaning of curiosity and consent.

Before attempting any of the following, it is helpful for a couple to have talked about them: contraception, safety of deep kissing, oral sex, anal sex, sex toys, limits on both bondage and discipline play or sadism and masochism play, coital positions, and introducing other partners into their sexual relationship. Each person needs to feel that all choices are consensual, out of sight and sound of unwilling observers, safe, and not hurtful to anyone involved. They need to explore the possible consequences of any of their sexual activities.

The Sexual and Erotic Response Cycles

Few writers approach sexual function from the perspective of similarity. In Chapter 3, I discussed male and female development from the same embryonic precursors. In terms of sexual function, both females and males are sexually biphasic, that is, both have a vasocongestive (swelling of genitals and breasts) and orgasmic phase in sexual arousal. Engorgement takes place in both sexes during arousal: in the female, of the labia, clitoris, and orgasmic platform inside the vagina: in the male, the penis and testicles. During the orgasm phase, both have eight to ten contractions per second in the sexual organs. Extragenital responses, such as nipple erection, possible skin flush, increased heart rate and respiratory rate, and involuntary reaction of face and body are also similar.

Psychologically, both females and males exercise their sexuality to express affection, release tension, and experience sexual response, which may or may not include orgasm, and possibly to create new life. Both females and males react to performance demands or fears with anxiety. The cause of much sexual dissatisfaction is anxiety occurring at various points in the response cycle. "Spectatoring" is a common phenomenon in both sexes, that is, at the point of anxiety the person steps out of the role of participant and becomes an observer. At times they also conjure up as their critical observer a parent, God, or a dead relative. An obsessive person is particularly likely to display this behavior. An unsatisfactory response usually results. Both females and males tend to avoid anxiety-producing situations; thus lack of interest or other avoidance techniques become defenses against getting into a sexual situation in which anxiety would be experienced. However, females and males react differently to anxiety. In the male, anxiety may make erection difficult or hastens sexual response, especially orgasm, whereas in the female anxiety delays or even inhibits arousal or orgasm.

Socially, people of all genders "fall in love," a condition characterized by intense preoccupation with the loved one, which either ceases or evolves into a long-term caring relationship with or without sexual attraction and interaction. Both sexes can respond erotically to symbolic representation, such as a photograph, drawing, mental picture, sexy film, body part or familiar gesture.

Certain characteristics have also been traditionally seen as male or female, such as being aggressive and dominant as male and being passive and a biologically-based nurturer as female. These, however, are culturally determined, and are beginning to be relaxed, allowing far more freedom for individual development. Ironically, the breaking down of these stereotypes has played a part in inducing sexual problems—for instance, in the man who has difficulty accepting an assertive female partner. Unfortunately, straight people often believe this stereotype, asking a gay and lesbian couple: "Who is the man and who is the woman?" Fortunately, these stereotypical roles are experienced less in the gay culture.

Understanding Sexual and Erotic Response

There have been many great contributions to our understanding of sexual pleasure emerging from the medical and behavioral sciences. There are three major contributions which to me are foundation stones for understanding the natural function of sexual pleasure and its theological significance. First, in the 1960s, William Masters and Virginia Johnson, of Washington University Medical School in St. Louis, can be credited with beginning the movement towards understanding the physiology of human sexual functioning. As a result of their groundbreaking research published in their book *Human Sexual Response* (1966), they were also instrumental in describing the problems that occur when the physiological system is blocked from functioning. They describe the sexual problems, their etiology and treatment, in their second book on *Human Sexual Inadequacy* (1970).

Masters and Johnson divided the sexual response cycle into four phases: excitement (or arousal), plateau, orgasm, and resolution. In their first book, they described in detail each of these phases in both the female and male. Both are born sexual and sexual responses occur from before birth until death. "Both vaginal lubrication and penile erections are based on sexual reflexes, which are biologically built into the body's neural and cardiovascular systems" (Baldwin & Baldwin, 2012).

While still in utero, females vaginally lubricate and males have erections. Interestingly, our grand daughter-in-law sent us a sonogram picture of our great grandson during her third trimester and it clearly showed him with an erection. Her comment was "you can tell we are going to have a Stayton boy." This phenomenon occurs while males and females are asleep, every 40-80 minutes, until death, unless interrupted by disease or chemical interventions. If human beings respond sexually from before birth until death, then this has important implications for our understanding of our development as sexual beings with the potential for sexual pleasure as a natural part of our lives.

The fact that sexual response is pleasurable has theological implications. It could be said that the Creator, or whoever is our ultimate Thou, intends sexual pleasure for the human creature. For example, females have an organ, the clitoris, which has no other function than for sexual pleasure. It has nothing to do with procreation or urination. While it has an analog in the penis, the penis has other functions such as urination and as a way of transmitting sperm. We should use the female, not the male, as the model for pleasure. Pleasure is pleasure and procreation is for procreation. The one does not have to go with the other, unless procreation is what is desired. If sexual pleasure was intended only for procreational purposes within the marriage bond, then God has played a terrible joke on the multitudes throughout history who never married or could not have children, or who theoretically could have had over 30 children during their child-bearing years! Must not our religious belief system take into account the fact that we have the capacity to experience sexual pleasure at birth and that sexual pleasure can be experienced until death?

In the late 1970s, Dr. Helen Singer Kaplan of Cornell University Medical School proposed an important fifth phase to the sexual response cycle, which precedes the original four. She called this the desire phase. She found that people could be blocked from sexual pleasure and response before excitement or arousal could take place.

Such people have an aversion to sex and to sexual pleasure. So Dr. Kaplan did a study of the components of sexual desire. She wrote this up in a very helpful book, *Disorders of Sexual Desire* (1979). Among the causes of a lack of desire were such factors as childhood trauma, child sexual abuse, rape, negative attitudes, low self-esteem, guilt, shame, and religious orthodoxy that repressed sexual expression. It is amazing to me how many people I have counseled that suffer from a lack of sexual desire who blame their problem on their religious upbringing. To me this is an indictment of religious belief systems that have failed to take into account a theology of sexual pleasure or even a religious affirmation of sexual expression other than for procreational purposes.

Another important contribution to our understanding the psychological nature of sexual response was proposed first by a friend and colleague of mine at the University of Pennsylvania and Jefferson Medical College in Philadelphia, Dr. David M. Reed. While he never published his theory, in my judgment it is crucial to understanding the importance of sexual pleasure. He called this theory ESP, or the theory of Erotic Stimulus Pathway, not to be confused with Extra-Sensory Perception. Dr. Reed proposed that sexual response was more than a physical and chemical matter. The real sex organ is not the genitals, but rather what is between the ears—the brain. He describes ESP in four phases, which cover the Kaplan and Masters and Johnson five phase model, as follows: seduction, sensations, surrender, and reflection.

This model is based upon a theory of psychosexual development. When people begin to date, they are experiencing the first stage of ESP, the Seduction phase. This important stage has two components: first, seducing oneself into being interested in another person, and second, learning how to seduce the other person into being interested in you. For young people this stage is enough in itself.

For example, I will never forget my first date. I can remember how excited I was when my 7th grade classmates told me that Julie liked me. I can remember how that relationship progressed during the 7th grade. We used to send notes to each other, then we started talking on the telephone to each other, and finally she invited me to the end-of-the-year dance. It was a formal dance. The time I spent picking out my clothes, taking a long bath, getting ready, and combing my hair even amazed my parents. Then, even though I was only 12 years old, I went to the medicine cabinet in our bathroom and splashed a lot of my father's Old Spice aftershave lotion on my face. My father drove us to the dance and picked us up. It was a wonderful evening—in fact it was perfect! There was no sex—I am not sure that I really even knew much about sex then, but it was a very important learning experience. I was developing the art of seduction, which later would play a vital part in sexual pleasure. I still think of that wonderful date whenever I wear Old Spice.

The next phase is the Sensations phase. Our senses are nature's aphrodisiacs. They are all that a person needs to gain and maintain sexual arousal and pleasure. The importance of touch, vision, hearing, smell, and taste cannot be overstated. Touch is a chief means of healing and pleasure, but all too often, touch becomes a way of controlling and punishing. Then it becomes abusive and a person so abused will have great difficulty in deriving pleasure from this very important sense. Seeing and hearing one's beloved and the sight and sound of sex can be very stimulating unless one is taught that the body is gross and the sounds of sex are frightening. The smell and taste of sex also stimulate, unless one has been told the smell is bad and to taste sex is wrong because the sexual organs are dirty. As a sex therapist I have learned how important the senses are to helping a couple with sexual problems. The fewer senses the couple uses, the more difficult it will be to help them become functional. Sexual function depends on sexual pleasure and that pleasure is based on our sensations. Yet do we impart this knowledge to our children?

The third phase in ESP is called the Surrender phase. For orgasm to take place as a pleasurable experience, one needs to let go and give control over to the experience. If one has been taught to be over-controlled or there are power struggles in the relationship, then the psychophysiological response will be affected. This can be hard for females who have been taught to play the "gate-keeper" role to keep things from "going too far." Even when happily in a good relationship, it can be hard to just surrender and let go to their arousal and pleasure.

The fourth and final phase, the Reflection phase, is most important. How a person feels immediately after the sexual experience will act as feedback to future sexual experiences with that person. If the immediate reflection is positive— that is, warm, loving, pleasurable—then the desire will be stimulated for the next time. If, on the other hand, the reflection is negative, i.e. the person did not like the way they experienced their response, or is negative about the partner or the situation, then the feedback will act to lower desire for the next time. The diagram below is how various phases fit together.

Sexual & Erotic Response Cycle

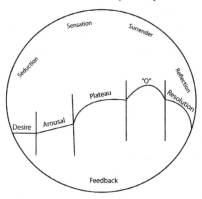

Fig. 3 Masters and Johnson, Kaplan, and Reed/Stayton Models

A common problem in long term relationships is that couples forget the importance of the seduction phase and go right for the sensations or orgasm phase. An example is the couple who lets sex go until the last experience of an already busy day just before going to sleep. When this occurs over time, then even the sensations begin to lose their power, and arousal is minimal. It is interesting that in working with couples involved in extramarital affairs, one of the major experiences that makes the extramarital affair exciting is that the seduction phase is reintroduced into a relationship. Keeping seduction alive in a long term relationship is vitally important and should be taught as part of a person's preparation for marriage.

Again, it is impressive how important sexual pleasure is in human relationships and sexual function. Yet how often do we prepare our children or help adults within the context of religion to experience the fullness of our Creator's intention for sexual pleasure? Where is a belief system that incorporates this important aspect of life?

When There are Sexual Problems

When there are sexual problems in a relationship, the individuals should be carefully screened to rule out neurological or biochemical causes. Lethargy, pain and depression from any systemic debilitating illness may affect one's interest in sex. It is important to talk over with one's physician the sexual side effects from surgery, endocrine disorders, neurological disorders, and medications prescribed for physical, psychological or psychiatric disorders.

Many drugs interfere with sexual performance. Alcohol, barbiturates, opiates, or opioids may seem to produce a transitory increased interest in sex, but all act as a depressant in the longer term. Hallucinogens and stimulants produce varying results, but in the addicted individual, they usually severely inhibit sexual functioning. Androgen increases libido in both sexes. Estrogen and progesterone do not enhance libido and in large doses may be inhibiting. Approximately 80 percent of persons with a sex problem suffer from significant relationship difficulties. Hostility and/or repressed anger are the most common component and is rarely compatible with intimate caring feelings.

Although sexual attitudes and behaviors appear to be changing, there is great disparity between idealized love and commercialized sex. Individuals are forced to determine sexual boundaries in the context of widespread sexual ignorance. Severe religious orthodoxy and moralism have contributed guilt, shame, fear, and the denial of sex as pleasure. As a result, sexual inhibition exists as a cultural baseline.

The feminist movements have challenged sex-role stereotypes; consequently, traits that were assigned to gender, such as passivity and aggressiveness, are now recognized as significantly determined by culture. Cultural imprinting or conditioning is considered an important cause of sexual problems. For example, I treated several couples where their sexual problems derived from the fact that the female was making significantly more money in her work than her male partner, who was brought up to believe that the role of the male was to be the major wage earner in the family. In one couple, the male stayed home to care for the children while the female was employed with a lucrative salary, as a professional in a law firm. While the couple felt they could make the adjustment, the judgments from family, neighbors, friends, all created problems in their sexual relationship, as did the long hours working in her law firm.

I have listed only a few of the potential problem areas in a sexual relationship, whereas each couple is unique in their presentation of their sexual problem, and while there are many good books and magazine articles describing the causes and cures for sexual problems, I will offer what I have found helpful in working with thousands of individuals and couples over my fifty years of practice.

First of all, Dr. Jack Anon, from the University of Hawaii, suggested in 1976 a model for the behavioral treatment of sexual needs and concerns of clients and when to make appropriate referrals. What he termed PLISSIT is an acronym for four stages of helping persons with sexual problems: Permission giving, Limited Information, Specific Suggestions, and Intensive Therapy.

Permission-giving is not the same as telling the patient what to do. Permission is usually for thoughts, feelings, or behaviors and may be expressed as permission to do or not to do. Permission-giving from a knowledgeable professional figure is quite powerful. This is not to give permission for thoughts, feelings, or behaviors that violate a person's value system. Rather it is to relieve guilt and shame from thoughts and acts that produce pleasure and satisfaction. For example, if a person is brought up with the idea that outside of marriage, sex is unhealthy, dirty, and sinful, it may be difficult to suddenly switch that idea after marriage. This can lead to the Madonna/Whore syndrome, mentioned earlier. Permission giving by a doctor, therapist, clergy, or other person considered as authority, can be helpful in breaking away from this syndrome.

Limited information-giving usually involves discussing anatomy and physiology and the sexual response cycle, as well as dispelling myths about sex. Sexual myths are common and need to be identified, understood and dispelled. For example, this book was designed to bring the reader knowledge about anatomy, physiology, behaviors, and religious belief systems and their effect on sexual relationships.

Specific suggestions involve skill-building, such as changing position for sexual activities, trying different sexual behaviors, using lubricants, considering sex toys, and enhanced techniques for love-making. An exercise that is often helpful is asking the couple, individually, to look at a book, such as, Paul Joannides, PsyD, *Guide to Getting It On!* (2015), go over the Table of Contents and list items (1) they like or want to do; (2) they are curious and want to learn more; and (3) activities they don't like or want to explore at all. I then take their lists to see what to explore in offering specific suggestions. I will cover later in this chapter the specific suggestions that I have found helpful in working with couples.

Intensive therapy may be necessary for body-image problems, working with persons with different abilities, relationship problems, identity issues, depression, personality disorders, or psychoses, or internalized homophobia, which can affect people coming out as LGBTQ. It is important to find the right therapist for the above issues. One source for such referrals is the American Association of Sexuality Educators, Counselors and Therapists. Consult www.aasect.org for a list of certified sex counselors and therapists.

Sensate Focus Exercises

When I began my postdoctoral work in sexuality and religion at the University of Pennsylvania, I was exposed to a group of sexually explicit films of individuals and couples, not actors or actresses, made by the Glide Memorial Methodist Church in San Francisco. My task was to find out whether viewing these films could be of help to our clients at Marriage Council of Philadelphia, now the Council for Relationships. We invited three groups of individuals and couples to a weekend of just watching the films and discussing their reactions. The three groups were: couples with severe sexual dysfunctions, a random sample of couples from the community without sexual problems, and a couples' group from a Baptist church in a small community in New Jersey. The films represented messages about sex, self-pleasuring (masturbation), same-sex couples, heterosexual couples, aging couples, and couples with a disability. The fact they were made by a Methodist Church was an important message to the participants. It was a form of religious permission-giving for viewing these films. We pre- and post-tested the client participants on attitudes, knowledge, behavior, and self-image. Six weeks after the last group, we brought together all thirty couples. The evaluations of the individuals and test results were consistently positive in each of the tested areas. In fact, most of the participants wished they had gone through this program earlier in their relationship, that their parents had gone through such a process, that their children could go through the program, and that therapists, clergy and doctors could have such an experience. As a result, the program, named Sexual Attitude Reassessment (SAR) has become required for anyone seeking certification, from AASECT, as a sexuality educator, counselor, or therapist. For many years I offered SAR programs at various seminaries around the country, including Roman Catholic, Protestant, and Jewish seminaries.

After my postdoctoral year, I joined the faculty at the university and was given the task of seeing how we might use explicit films in helping individuals and couples in sex therapy. I was sent to St. Louis to learn from Masters and Johnson about working with couples. I was sent to California to learn the methods of Hartman and Fithian, who exposed couples with sexual problems to viewing sexually functional couples through explicit sexual films. I was sent to the University of Indiana (the Kinsey Institute) to learn their methods.

During this same time, sex therapy films were released to illustrate simple pleasuring exercises to increase or enhance the arousal process. Masters and Johnson called these exercises "sensate focus." First, the couple sensually touch each other over their entire bodies, except for the genital and breast areas. This is often difficult, because when the couple is experiencing sexual difficulties, one or both often take on spectator roles and try to think about what is going on in their partner's head. They lose the focus on their own pleasure as participants.

Once partners have been able to focus on their own pleasurable experiences, they can explore the breasts and genitals and determine which touches are pleasurable, threatening, or irritating. What many couples do not realize is that different areas on the body, breasts and genitals can be more erotic and sensitive than other spots. Next, the couple caresses the breasts and genitals to produce arousal. If either or both of the partners experience arousal, they may go on to orgasm, with or without intercourse. Further sensate focus exercises can be helpful to couples in exploring different positions for intercourse, whether vaginal or anal. While I have used these videos in many religious institutions, it remains to be seen whether they will be accepted in the majority of religious settings. I have yet to have a couple decide not to view them as a part of therapy or a couple who have not found them helpful. A list of resources for getting the Sensate Focus videos can be found at the end of this chapter.

Hopefully, the reader has seen how important the framework for viewing sexuality through one's deeply held beliefs, cultural and sexual value systems is to the formation of one's feelings, attitudes and behaviors. It was also important to understand the development of morality and moral behavior in assessing the modern sexuality dilemmas facing our and our children's generation.

Now that the intersections between the biological, psychological, social, and sexual aspects of being human have been covered, it is important to take a new look at the Bible and what it may really say about sexuality.

RESOURCES
Sensate Focus Videos

There are many excellent sensate focus films that are available today. A great resource for sexually related films is www.sexsmartfilms.com.

Because, all too often, the sensate focus films have represented only heterosexual couples, it was my dream to have films for lesbian and gay couples, as well as straight couples who represent diversity. As a member of the Health Science Advisory Board of WebPower, a computer software development company, I was given a grant to make sensate focus films for lesbian, gay and straight couples. These films, called "A Guide to Sexual Pleasure," use non-professional couples of different ages, and include African-American, Hispanic (Latinx), and Caucasian persons. They are available, in part, on the SexSmartFilms website. The full set of videos are on the website: www.drstayton.com. These videos give descriptions of male and female anatomy as well as the sexual and erotic response cycle. They are narrated by both sex educators and therapists. On my website each segment offers suggestions before and after viewing each sensate focus exercise. There are also common questions from clients and answers provided by professional therapists relevant to gay, lesbian and straight couples. The films were produced and directed by Dr. Mark Schoen, a professional filmmaker.

Chapter 8

SEXUALITY AND THE BIBLE

As I begin this chapter on Sexuality and the Bible, I think it is important to put the Bible in an evolutionary perspective, which unfortunately I think is rare among religious people. Because of newer archeological findings and carbon dating, this information was not even available when I went to seminary.

The Abrahamic religions (Hebrew, Christian, and Islam) are a late development in the evolution of religions coming around 1800 to 1500 BCE with Moses. As mentioned in an earlier chapter, according to Genesis, not only was Eve created from Adam's body, she tempted Adam to eat from the forbidden fruit and thus was the cause of their expulsion from the Garden of Eden. Yet what may be new to many is that as early as 37,000 BCE, there were religions around the world based around the female and female deities. Archeological evidence illustrates there were Goddesses throughout the world. In the Near and Middle East female deities were named Queen of Heaven. There are many accounts of female Creators, who not only created the heavens and earth, but brought forth the first humans;

she was the source of all being. In the Middle East God-dess religions existed and flourished for thousands of years, long before the arrival of Moses and Abraham with their male deity and patriarchy. From ancient art, archeological excavations, and sculptures we learn that the female religions around the world honored nature, birthing, sensuality, pleasure, peace, relationships, and sexuality. Evolutionarily women were also responsible for the development of planting, agriculture, harvesting, and food gathering methods. This history of the Goddesses and their cultures were both fascinating and blew my mind. (To get further information, I would suggest Merlin Stone (1976), *When God was a Woman*; Marietta Now (1980), *Eve's Rib: A Revolutionary New View of the Female*; and Riane Eisler (1995), *The Chalice and the Blade*.)

For centuries it was not even known that males had a role in procreation. Sex was there only for pleasure. While it is clear that at first the Goddesses reigned alone, there came a point where the male was introduced through being her brother or son, but then became her lover and spouse. In the beginning, she had priority of importance over the Young-god who became her son or husband or lover. According to Merlin Stone, "It was this youth who symbolized the male role in the sacred annual sexual union with the Goddess" (pg. 19). To many people today this information may be dismissed as heathenism. The Merriam-Webster dictionary defines heathen as "one who has little or no religion and who delights in sensual pleasures." To me this illustrates how a positive view of sexuality and sensuality was found in the female religions which existed long before the sex-negativity often found in the male dominated Abrahamic religions.

According to Stone, "The Northern Invaders (15,000 – 8,000), generally known as Indo-European, brought their own religion with them, the worship of a young warrior god and/or supreme father god. Their arrival is archaeologically and historically attested to by 2,400 BCE. Evidence indicates that matriarchy and patriarchy existed as side-by-side partners and equals for several thousand years until patriarchy was established in religious and civil laws" (pg. 20). Stone's book is replete with stories that link the destruction of the Goddess religions in the Bible and final dominance of the male over the female. With this important brief context, I begin my review of sexuality and the Bible.

Years ago, a group of evangelical students in my University of Pennsylvania classroom said during the semester that I had stepped on every one of their sexual values and what they were taught about what the Bible teaches about sex. They further questioned how a minister could teach this course and deviate so much from the Bible's messages. I was shocked because I believe that our sexual values are sacred and I do not want to step on anyone's values. I felt they had a total misunderstanding of the Bible. I suggested they bring a Bible to class the following week. I said that after looking at the Bible, we would look at differing sexual value systems within religions and our culture.

I started the following class with a bit of trivia to get at some important knowledge. See what your answers would be. The answers will be at the end of this chapter. These questions sound trivial, but they do have relevance to how the Bible came into being and to the meaning that can be extracted from it, as the reader will see by the end of this chapter.

- How many books are there in the Bible?

- When were the books of the Bible divided into chapters?

- When were verse divisions introduced into the Bible?

- How many verses are there in the entire Bible?

- How many Bible translations are there in English?

- How many verses are there in the Bible on the following subjects:

  Same-sex sexual behavior?
  Condoning and supporting slavery?
  Poverty, injustice and serving others?

What is the Bible?

There are numerous books in the Bible and a good many more candidate books were excluded. While we don't know the authors of the majority of the books, we have several working theories. The first five books of the Bible are known as the Torah: Genesis, Exodus, Leviticus, Numbers, and Deuteronomy. The Torah is the body of wisdom and law for the Jewish people, along with other sacred literature and oral tradition, the Mishnah and Talmud. While they are called the Books of Moses, we know that Moses did not write anything that still exists today.

It is believed that there are at least five author groups for the Torah. They are called: J (standing for the use of Yahweh as the name for God), E (standing for those verses that use Elohim for God), D (the books of Deuteronomy and Numbers which are the source of most of the Hebrew laws in the Torah), and P (standing for the priestly writers, who are most concerned with rituals and ceremonies). When I was in seminary, I had to go through and underline with different colored pencils the verses thought to be derived from each of these four sources.

Following the Torah are the Historical books. Then the Prophets and Wisdom Literature, followed by the Apocrypha, which are the intertestamental books of history between the ending of the Hebrew Bible (or Old Testament) and the writings in the Christian Testament (or New Testament). The Apocrypha, while included in some but not all Bibles, is followed by the Christian Testament (New Testament) and the Apocalyptic literature, consisting of the books of Daniel and Revelation. Most of the above books probably have multiple authors.

Problems of Translation

Of considerable significance is the fact that there are several problems in biblical translation. First, there have been numerous translations. The earliest translators were scribes, who would spend their entire career translating a small portion of scripture. There are Bibles translated by committees who gather Hebrew, Greek, Aramaic, and Latin scriptures together and vote on what they believe is the best translation of various parts of scripture. There are numerous committee versions of the Bible, both Roman Catholic and Protestant versions. Finally, there are also many versions of the Bible that have been translated by individuals. One factor that has to be kept in mind is that all versions are also written in a particular sociopolitical climate.

The second problem in translation is that sentences in the original Hebrew and Aramaic languages do not have either vowels or word breaks.

Ltthddbrythdd

An example, in English, is the following verse from Matthew 8:22 and Luke 9:60. Without looking up those verses, can you translate this verse? The difficulty of doing so should be very instructive. The answer is at the end of this chapter.

Third, the meaning of words has changed over the centuries. Using today's word definitions can be very misleading. There is also the fact that words can have various meanings depending on the context and/or declension. For example, the word "relative" could mean 1) a relationship, or 2) being relevant or comparative. Following are some biblical words that are subject to mistranslation:

Virgin—a. One who has never had sexual intercourse. b. One who is usually a female. c. But are there not also male virgins? This is not addressed in the scriptures. d. A woman of marriageable age who has never had sexual intercourse. e. A woman of marriageable age, whether or not she has had sexual interaction with her intended spouse.

The correct answer for most biblical scholars is "e".

Abomination—a. Any sexual behavior regarded with disgust or hatred. b. Any sexual behavior regarded with disgust or hatred in the Torah. c. Food made from unclean creatures that are not to be eaten. Example: fowl such as wild birds, chicken, turkey, etc. d. Any foreign gods or improper ways of worshipping God. e. Any unacceptable or unlawful conduct as found in the Bible. f. In the book of Proverbs are more secular uses, in which something is described not as an abomination to God, but to others. g. The act of desecrating the Temple in Jerusalem (Daniel).

The correct answer is all, depending on which books of the Bible are being quoted.

Adultery—In this century the word has to do with anyone who has sex with a married person. In the Bible, this word is basically an economic term meaning anyone who violates another man's property rights. Women were part of a man's property. However, if the owner of the property, such as a husband, gave permission to a visiting friend, for example, to have sex with one of his wives, it would not be considered adultery.

Fornication—In the Torah, sexual behaviors with any relative or members of the relative's family, bestiality, rape, or members of the same sex are considered fornication. This helps to keep family relationships free from any detrimental effects of inbreeding, such as economic inheritance. Fornication is also about any sexual behaviors that are practiced in any of the communities that the Israelites were traveling through, such as same-sex behaviors and ritual "prostitution". In the Christian Testament (New Testament) almost any form of sexual activity outside of marriage was considered fornication.

Feet—The Hebrew word for feet can also mean genitals or lower part of the body, as well as feet and toes, which is an interesting aspect when it comes to the washing of feet in the Bible. Foot washing can also be very sensual, which for many may lead to sexual arousal. It can be a very intimate experience. (Luke 7: 36-50; John 13: 1-16).

Ways of Approaching the Bible
As I told my students, there are at least four different ways of approaching one's reading of the Bible:

- The Bible is evil, harmful, and can cause war. Throughout history religion and scripture have been at the
  center of conflict and war. There are those who see no
  good coming from the Bible. While it can be fun to
  debate this subject, it was not the concern of any of
  my students.

- The Bible has great historical and literary value. When
  I was in college, I had a course that offered this perspective. This view argues that the Bible is a good
  history of a group of people, their accomplishments,
  teachings and conflicts that gives us different perspectives of this period of history. Depending on the translation, there is poetry that is unsurpassed in literature,
  which also gives a historical perspective on events
  and persons (Psalms, Song of Solomon as examples).
  Again, it is interesting to discuss this perspective on
  the Bible, but it was not the issue brought up by my
  students.

- There is the literalist who says: "The Bible is the Word
  of God, directly from God, and every word is true."
  This was the perspective of some of my students and
  the point of my class that day. As an example, I asked
  them for an explanation for the following scriptural
  verses:

First, we started with the Hebrew Bible (Old Testament).
The following is a sample of the many purity laws. All
quotes are from the New Revised Standard Version of the
Bible, a common version currently used in many Protestant
churches.

Leviticus 15: 16-33. "If a man has an emission of semen, he shall bathe his whole body in water, and be unclean.... Everything made of cloth or of skin on which the semen falls shall be washed with water, and be unclean...Everything upon which she lies...Whoever touches her bed... Whoever touches anything upon which she sits...If any man lies with her , and her impurity falls on him, he shall be unclean..."

This portion of scripture has to do with the products of menstruation and male sperm, the touching or sleeping with a menstruating woman. I have had Orthodox Jewish patients and students who hold to this view, but the rest of my students did not. The literalists generally give a view that because of our views on cleanliness and healthy practice today, this passage is no longer relevant. They also shared the view that this is the law of the Old Testament and Jesus brought a new law that supersedes the old law. This becomes an important point that my literalist students continued to voice.

Leviticus 20: 18. "If a man lies with a woman having her sickness and uncovers her nakedness...both of them shall be cut off from their people."

Deuteronomy 22: 5. "A woman shall not wear a man's apparel, nor shall a man put on a woman's garment; for whoever does such things is abhorrent to the Lord your God." While many agree with the part that men should not wear women's clothes, there is a lot of disagreement about women wearing male type clothing, such a pants, shirts, coats, etc.

Deuteronomy 23: 1. "No one whose testicles are crushed or whose penis is cut off shall be admitted to the assembly of the Lord." This clearly became an issue when soldiers who had stepped on an "improvised explosive device" (IED) and lost their penis and/or testicles or men who develop cancer of the testicles and had one or both removed.

Deuteronomy 23: 2. "Those born of an illicit union shall not be admitted to the assembly of the Lord. Even to the tenth generation none of their descendants shall be admitted to the assembly of the Lord." Most of the students believed that this would outlaw most people as none were able to go back 10 generations in their own family to ascertain that all were legitimate.

Deuteronomy 24: 5. "When a man is newly married, he shall not go out with the army or be charged with any related duty. He shall be free at home one year to be happy with the wife whom he has married." Most of the students had never heard of this verse and agreed it was not a bad idea!

While both Jewish and Christian people consider parts of the Torah relevant, by this time in class, most felt they got the message that many laws of the Torah are not relevant today, so it was time to start with the New Testament.

Ephesians 5: 22-24. "Wives, be subject to your husbands as you are to the Lord. For the husband is the head of the wife just as Christ is the head of the church, the body of which he is the Savior. Just as the church is subject to Christ, so also wives ought to be, in everything, to their husbands." It was noted that these verses have been used in many court cases to support spousal rape and abuse on religious grounds.

Ephesians 6: 5-8. "Slaves, obey your earthly masters with fear and trembling, in singleness of heart, as you obey Christ; not only while being watched, and in order to please them, but as slaves of Christ, doing the will of God from the heart. Render service with enthusiasm, as to the Lord and not to men and women, knowing that whatever good we do, we will receive the same again from the Lord, whether we are slaves or free." These verses were used to support slavery, even by many churches and some denominations, for centuries.

I Corinthians 14: 34-35. "As in all the churches of the saints, women should be silent in the churches. For they are not permitted to speak, but should be subordinate, as the law also says. . .For it is shameful for a woman to speak in church." It was noted that there are very few churches and synagogues today where women are not involved in the life of a congregation, on committees, in the religious education program, as well as on the staff. Today, of course, women and persons who are transgender are serving as ministers and rabbis.

I Timothy 2: 9-15. "The women should dress themselves modestly and decently in suitable clothing, not with their hair braided, or with gold, pearls, or expensive clothes, but with good works, as is proper for women who profess reverence for God. . .Yet she will be saved through childbearing, provided they continue in faith and love and holiness, with modesty."

Because no one in class could go along with any or all of the above scriptural examples, it became clear that there is no such person as a literalist in accepting that every word of the Bible is true and comes from God.

An issue that arose was how can the laws of a perfect Being (God) ever be construed as being imperfect? A perfect Being cannot change. If it does, it can only be in the direction of imperfection. Hence, any law held at any time to be a law of God must be perfect and cannot be updated or changed in any way. To hold that God's laws are changeable is to admit that either God is not perfect, or that God's laws are, in fact, not God's at all, but are of human origin.

This brought us to the fourth way of approaching the Bible, that of the contextualist who says we need to understand what the writer was really saying and to whom, what is the historical context, and what relevance, if any, it may have for us today.

The Clobber Passages: Looking at the Context

Clobber passages are verses from the Bible that are used by those who are against certain sexual issues and behaviors to clobber those who are supportive of and/or speaking on behalf of those same sexual issues and behaviors. To take on all of the sexually related scriptures could be a book in itself, so just one topic will be considered in this chapter.

The topic of homosexuality is a major concern in our society today. There are only six references in the entire Bible used to clobber those who are proponents and supportive of homosexuality. Some other sexuality-related scriptures will be taken up in other chapters as they are relevant.

The first reference is Genesis 19: 1-11. (There is a similar story in Judges 19: 16-30) The Genesis story is the well-known story of Sodom and Gomorrah.

"…two angels (messengers) came to Sodom in the evening, and Lot was sitting in the gateway of Sodom. When Lot saw them, he rose to meet them, and bowed down with his face to the ground. He said, 'Please, my lords, turn aside to your servant's house and spend the night, and wash your feet; then you can rise early and go on your way.' They said, 'No; we will spend the night in the street.' But he urged them strongly; so they turned aside to him and entered his house; and he made them a feast, and baked unleavened bread, and they ate. But before they lay down, the men of the city, the men of Sodom both young and old, all the people to the last man, surrounded the house; and they call to Lot, 'Where are the men who came to you tonight? Bring them out to us, so that we may *know* them.' Lot went out of the door to the men, shut the door after him, and said, 'I beg you, my brothers, do not act so wickedly. Look, I have two daughters who have not known a man; let me bring them out to you, and do to them as you please; only do nothing to these men, for they have come under the shelter of my roof.' But they replied, 'Stand back!' And they said, 'This fellow came here as an alien, and he would play the judge! Now we will deal worse with you than with them.' Then they pressed hard against the man Lot, and came near the door to break it down. But the men inside reached out their hands and brought Lot into the house with them, and shut the door. And they struck with blindness the men who were at the door of the house, both small and great, so that they were unable to find the door."

Some interesting things to note about this story is first, the word "know" which is translated in different biblical texts as rape, have sex, have intercourse, have intimacies, know, or know them as well. Second, the Hebrew word used here is found in the Old Testament 953 times as "to know," as in get acquainted with. Only 10 times does the word mean to have sex and each time it is only associated with heterosexual sex. Third, the sins of Sodom and Gomorrah are referred to only in four other biblical passages:

Jeremiah 23: 14. "…they commit adultery and walk in lies; they strengthen the hands of evildoers, so that no one turns from wickedness; all of them have become like Sodom to me, and its inhabitants like Gomorrah."

Ezekiel 16: 49-50. "This was the guilt of your sister Sodom: she and her daughters had pride, excess of food, and prosperous ease, but did not aid the poor and needy. They were haughty, and did abominable things before me."

Matthew 10: 14-15. Jesus says, "If anyone will not welcome you or listen to your words, shake off the dust from your feet as you leave that house or town. Truly I tell you, it will be tolerable for the land of Sodom and Gomorrah on the day of judgment than for that town."

Luke 10: 10-12. Jesus says "But whenever you enter a town and they do not welcome you, go out into the streets and say, 'Even the dust of your town that clings to our feet, we wipe off in protest against you. Yet know this: the kingdom of God has come near.' I tell you, on that day it will be more tolerable for Sodom than for that town."

In other words, nowhere in the Bible are Sodom and Gomorrah linked to sexual behavior, but rather to inhospitality, which has always been an important value in Hebrew religious practice. There is nothing in the Bible that links

Sodom and Gomorrah with same-sex sexual interaction. Even if it did, it would be about gang rape, rather than mutually agreed upon and consensual adult sexual behavior. The first extra-biblical reference to Sodom and Gomorrah being linked to same-sex behavior was Josephus, a first century Jewish historian, who hated the Romans and their acceptance of same-sex relationships.

The second and third passages relating to same-sex coupling are found in the Torah's Purity Code, whose purpose was to keep the Israelites pure from the influence of other cultures during their many years' journey from Egypt to Israel.

Leviticus 18: 22. "You shall not lie with a male as with a woman; it is an abomination."

Leviticus 20: 13. "If a man lies with a male as with a woman, both of them have committed an abomination; they shall be put to death; their blood is upon them."

What is behind these passages? We find the answer to this question in the following passage just a few verses ahead:

Leviticus 20: 22-24. "You shall keep all my statutes and all my ordinances, and observe them, so that the land to which I bring you to settle in may not vomit you out. You shall not follow the practices of the nation that I am driving out before you. Because they did all these things, I abhorred them. But I have said to you: You shall inherit their land, and I will give it to you to possess, a land flowing with milk and honey. I am the Lord your God; I have separated you from the peoples." The practices referred to were paganism, temple prostitution, as well as same and other sex behaviors that were part of rituals related to religious ceremonies.

The fourth and fifth clobber passages are from the New Testament, the interpretation of which again depends on language as translated from the original Greek.

I Corinthians 6: 9-10. "Do you not know that wrongdoers will not inherit the kingdom of God? Do not be deceived; neither the immoral, nor idolaters, not adulterers, nor homosexuals, nor thieves, nor the greedy, nor drunkards, nor revilers, nor robbers—will inherit the kingdom of God."

I Timothy 1: 9-10. "…the law is not laid down for the just but for the lawless and disobedient, for the ungodly and sinners, for the unholy and profane, for murders of fathers and murders of mothers, for manslayers, immoral persons, sodomites, kidnappers, liars, perjurers, and whatever else is contrary to sound doctrine ….."

There are two Greek words used in these scriptural passages that are not found elsewhere in the Greek language: malakoi and arsenokoitai. First malakoi, is translated in at least a dozen versions of the Bible as sissy or weakling, effeminate, catamites, self-indulgent, depraved, homosexual perverts, boy prostitutes, or male prostitutes. Second, arsenokoitai is translated separately as raper of boys, abusers of themselves with mankind, child-molesters, homosexuals, sodomites, persons of sordid morals, practicing homosexuals, or homosexual offenders.

In most other biblical translations the words are combined as guilty of homosexual perversion, sexual pervert, homosexuals, sexual perverts, male prostitutes, sodomites, homosexual perverts, hustlers, pederasts, or men and women who traffic human flesh. It is very important to note that there is *no equivalent word in Hebrew for "homosexual"*. This term was not used until the 19th century C.E., followed by the first use of the term "heterosexual". Both texts are presumably responses by Paul written in response to questions given to him. We do not have the texts of the letters asking the questions. Many scholars believe that the questions had to do with a common ancient Greek and Roman practice of "pederasty," which was being questioned at the time. Pederasty was the practice of an adult male who engaged in sexual activity with a male youth. It was a common practice for an adult male to be a mentor for a youth. The mentoring included teaching about economics, politics, history, religion, family, and sexuality, including engaging in sexual activity with the youth. The youth would then grow up, get married, and possibly become a mentor for other youths. The questioning of the churches could have been about the sexual abuses in this system. The Greek words used by Paul may have been slang terms used to describe this practice. While at the time of Jesus and Paul, it was an accepted practice, it came to be increasingly questioned and finally to be officially outlawed.

The final passage which for many is the most significant and troubling is the following:

Roman 1: 26-27. "For this reason God gave them up to dishonorable passions. Their women exchanged natural relations for unnatural, and the men likewise gave up natural relations with women and were consumed with passion for one another, men committing shameless acts with men and receiving in their own persons the due penalty for their error."

The book of Romans is the longest and considered to be the most theological of the letters attributed to Paul. His letters were written to both Jews and non-Jews (Gentiles), both of which groups were considered under the wrath of God and in need of salvation. Paul had been to both Corinth and Rome, and one might imagine that while staying in the "Rome Hilton" he would look across the way and see a Temple of Dionysus and would remember the Temple of Aphrodite. Both represented the worship of gods who celebrated wine, sex and fun. They were known for sexual orgies and for worshiping idols. These were the issues that Paul spoke out against in his letter to the Romans. In the verses stated above, Paul was targeting sexual practices performed in rituals that went against what he considered to be the natural order, as for example, straight men or women having sex with others of their own gender. It does not seem that he was speaking out against freely chosen sex partners; he was against idolatry and ritualized sex.

In conclusion, it is important and noteworthy that nowhere in the Gospels does Jesus speak against same gender sex. In the New Testament, the only same sex practices that Paul spoke about were pederasty (sexual activity between adults and youth) and religious rituals of sexual orgies. It should be noted that many New Testament scholars believe that some of the letters attributed to Paul were not written by him. While Romans and I Corinthians are not disputed as written by Paul, I Timothy is one of the Letters where it is questioned whether Paul was the author. It is also worth asking whether any of the Letters attributed to Paul's or any author's views on sexual matters should count as the uncontested word of God.

Responding to Those Who Oppose Homosexuality

When it comes to how to respond to those who oppose homosexuality, there seem to be three choices:

- To engage in what one might call a "pissing contest," i.e. to cite verses that support opposing views on the subject.

- To make Jesus the trump card, since he never addressed the subject of homosexuality in any of his teachings.

- To claim that homosexual people fit the glass slipper too. As examples, we may cite the love between Jonathan and David, Ruth and Naomi, Jesus and John, and the Eunuchs:

Jonathan and David—I Samuel 18: 3: "Then Jonathan made a covenant with David, because he loved him as his own soul."

Ruth and Naomi—Ruth, chapters 1-4: Ruth's vow to Naomi is a moving account similar to a covenant in marriage. The book of Ruth is a story of two women in love.

Jesus and John—John 13: 23: At the last supper, the issue of one of them denying Jesus was asked by the youngest disciple, John, "the one whom Jesus loved—was reclining next to him on his bosom." John describes himself as "the disciple whom Jesus loved." Another telling statement about their relationship was when Jesus was dying, he says in John 19: 26-27: "When Jesus saw his mother there, and the disciple whom he loved standing nearby, he said to his mother, 'Dear woman, here is your son,' and to the disciple, 'Here is your mother.' From that time on, this disciple took her into his home."

Eunichs—Matthew 19: 12: Evidently, there were many men, in Jesus' time, who did not take marriage seriously and took divorce too lightly. Jesus' disciples asked him "If such is the case of a man with his wife, it is better not to marry." Jesus gave an interesting response: "Not everyone can accept this teaching, but only those to whom it is given. For there are eunuchs who have been so from birth, and there are eunuchs who have been made eunuchs by others, and there are eunuchs who have made themselves eunuchs for the sake of the kingdom of heaven. Let anyone accept this who can."

In Biblical times, there was a poor understanding of biological sex, gender identity, and sexual orientation, and therefore, intersex persons, transgender persons, and persons with a different sexual orientation could have been classified under the term "eunuch," a special person. From this definition, it appears Jesus was prescribing tolerance and that there were three kinds of eunuchs. First, those made so from birth. This would cover intersex persons, those who had physical characteristics of both males and females. Today, for example, one out of every 2,000 live births is an intersex child. In Biblical times, there was no medical knowledge of or term for the condition. However, intersex children must have been seen as "special" persons. Second, there were eunuchs who were deliberately castrated. This was a common punishment for those who committed a crime, or was the fate of captives from another country or army. Thus, I think it is safe to say these would not be the persons in charge of harems or trusted with the treasury of a household or country. Third, there were those who were eunuchs by their own choosing. This does not necessarily imply surgical castration, but even if they were surgically castrated, it does not mean that they were not interested in sex. Persons who have had their testicles removed can still be interested in sex; they just cannot procreate. In Biblical times, it certainly meant that they were not interested in marriage or sex with a woman. These could be the "special" persons who were put in charge of a harem or trusted with the wives of a household. In today's world, a "gay" person would be a perfect choice for this biblical position.

Eunuchs are also held as special people in Isaiah 56: 3-5 and Acts 8: 27-39.

In view of all the ambiguities associated with biblical support either for or against homosexuality, the best response to those who oppose it for religious reasons may be to cite the separation of church and state guaranteed by the 1st Amendment of the Constitution. "Congress shall make no law respecting an establishment of religion, or prohibiting the free exercise thereof." This is such an important amendment because, in spite of many churches, the Supreme Court and Congress have given many protections allowing gay men and lesbians to marry, serve in the military, and not be discriminated against for employment. Based on all that has been said in this book, protecting sexual rights needs to be supported and protected, which can point our religions in new directions.

Answers to Trivia Questions & Biblical Verse example

- 66 Books: 39 in Hebrew Bible (Old Testament); 27 in Christian Testament (New Testament)

- Chapter Divisions: 1227 C.E. by the Archbishop of Canterbury

- Verse Divisions: Hebrew Bible (O.T.) 1448

- C.E. by Rabbi Nathan; Christian Testament (N.T.) 1555 C.E. by Robert Stephanus

- Bible Translations in English: $18^{th}/19^{th}$ century—9; 20th century—153; 21st century—5+

- Verses on particular subjects:

  - Same Gender Sex: 5 verses

  - Condoning and supporting Slavery: 67 verses

  - Poverty, Injustice and Serving others: 2000+ verses

- Translation of Hebrew verse in English: Matthew 8:22 & Luke 9:60

  - "Let the dead bury the dead"

- The translation of this verse makes no sense. However, in Hebrew, according to some biblical scholars, the same word for "dead" could mean "next of kin," which according to them makes more sense. "Let the next of kin bury the dead."

Chapter 9

UNIVERSAL
SEXUAL RIGHTS

In 1975, the World Health Organization (WHO) published the first international statement on sexuality. It read: "Sexual health is the integration of the somatic, emotional, intellectual, and social aspects of sexual being in ways that are positively enriching and that enhance personality, communication and love. Fundamental to this concept are the right to sexual information and the right to pleasure." Interestingly, one of the authors of this statement was the director of my first academic position at the University of Pennsylvania, Department of Psychiatry, Harold I. Lief, M.D., Ph.D. While it is a fine statement, by the 1990s, it needed to be updated.

There are critical sexual problems world-wide, including violence against women, unplanned pregnancies, sexual problems in relationships, sexually transmitted infections (including HIV/AIDS), abortion rates, and child sexual abuse and trafficking. In the early 1990s, the World Health Organization (WHO), and later, in 1998, our own U.S. Surgeon General David Satcher felt it important to make more than a statement and to take action.

First, the 1975 WHO implied sexual rights, but never articulated them. The World Association for Sexual Health (WAS) wanted to explore the question of whether there are universal sexual rights. WAS is a multidisciplinary, worldwide group of scientific societies, nongovernmental organizations (NGOs), and academics and professionals in the field of human sexuality. It promotes sexual health throughout the human lifespan and supports sexual rights for all people. WAS developed a Declaration of Sexual Rights that was first presented in Spain in 1997 and then ratified in Hong Kong in 1999. Since 1999 there has been one revision in 2012 ratified by the 2014 WAS General Assembly in Mexico City. The text of that declaration that follows is from https://worldsexualhealth.net/wp-content/uploads/2013/08/Declaration-of-Sexual-Rights-2014-plain-text.pdf.

World Association for Sexual Health Declaration of Sexual Rights

"In recognition that sexual rights are essential for the achievement of the highest attainable sexual health, the World Association for Sexual Health:

States that sexual rights are grounded in universal human rights that are already recognized in international and regional human rights documents, in national constitutions and laws, human rights standards and principles and in scientific knowledge related to human sexuality and sexual health.

Reaffirms that sexuality is a central aspect of being human throughout life, encompasses sex, gender identities and roles, sexual orientation, eroticism, pleasure, intimacy, and reproduction. Sexuality is experienced and expressed in thoughts, fantasies, desires, beliefs, attitudes, values, behaviors, practices, roles, and relationships. While sexuality can include all of these dimensions, not all of them are always experienced or expressed. Sexuality is influenced by the interaction of biological, psychological, social, economic, political, cultural, legal, historical, religious, and spiritual factors.

Recognizes that sexuality is a source of pleasure and wellbeing and contributed to overall fulfillment and satisfaction.

Reaffirms that sexual health is a state of physical, emotional, mental and social wellbeing in relation to sexuality; it is not merely the absence of disease, dysfunction or infirmity. Sexual health requires a positive and respectful approach to sexuality and sexual relationships, as well as their possibility of having pleasurable and safe sexual experiences, free of coercion, discrimination and violence.

Reaffirms that sexual health cannot be defined, understood or made operational without a broad understanding of sexuality.

Reaffirms that for sexual health to be attained and maintained, the sexual rights of all persons must be respected, protected and fulfilled.

Recognizes that sexual rights are based on the inherent freedom, dignity, and equality of all human beings and include a commitment to protection from harm.

States that equality and non-discrimination are foundational to all human rights protection and promotion and include the prohibition of any distinction, exclusion or restriction on the basis of race, ethnicity, color, sex, language, religion, political or other opinion, national or social origin, property, birth or other status, including disability, age, nationality, marital and family status, sexual orientation and gender identity, health status, place of residence, economic and social situation.

Recognizes that persons' sexual orientations, gender identities, gender expressions and bodily diversities require human rights protection.

Recognizes that all types of violence, harassment, discrimination, exclusion, and stigmatization are violations of human rights, and impact the wellbeing of individuals, families and communities.

Affirms that the obligations to respect, protect and fulfill human rights apply to all sexual rights and freedoms.

Affirms that sexual rights protect all people's rights to fulfill and express their sexuality and enjoy sexual health, with due regards for the rights of others."

In other words, the above recognitions and affirmations put forth the idea that human rights are also needed for advocating sexual rights!

World Association for Sexual Health
"Sexual Rights are Human Rights Pertaining to Sexuality:

1. The right to life, liberty, and security of the person.

2. The right to equality and non-discrimination.

3. The right to autonomy and bodily integrity.

4. The right to be free from torture and cruel, inhuman, or degrading treatment or punishment.

5. The right to be free from all forms of violence and coercion.

6. The right to the freedom of thought, opinion, and expression.

7. The right to privacy.

8. The right to the highest attainable standard of health, including sexual health; which implies the possibility of having pleasurable, satisfying, and safe sexual experiences.

9. The right to enjoy the benefits of scientific progress and its application.

10. The right to information.

11. The right to education and the right to comprehensive sexuality education.

12. The right to enter, form, and dissolve marriage and other types of relationships based on equality and full and free consent.

13. The right to whether to have children, the number and spacing of children, and to have the information and the means to do so.

14. The right to access to justice, remedies, and redress.

15. The right to freedom of association and peaceful assembly.

16. The right to participation in public and political
    life."

Basically, the Declaration of Sexual Rights affirmed the
universal central role that sexuality plays in all of human
life. Further, the WAS Declaration stated that equality for
all people must include no prohibitions based on difference.
Finally, WAS declared the above 16 universal sexual rights
that have been referred to the World Health Organization
(https://worldsexualhealth.net/2014).

Being aware that WHO and WAS were working on
the above sexual rights, the 16th US Surgeon General, Dr.
David Satcher, who was Surgeon General from 1998-2002,
decided that as the United States physician responsible for
public health issues, one of his major contributions would
be to develop *A Call to Action to Promote Sexual Health
and Responsible Sexual Behavior.* He developed a collaborative process, with persons from Health and Human
Services and the Office of Population Services, to engage
in scientific review of papers with experts from relevant
fields, representatives from the academic, medical and
religious communities, policy makers, advocates, teachers,
parents and youth. I was fortunate to have served on this
project. The purpose would be to begin a national dialogue
on sexuality, sexual health, and responsible sexual behavior. Dr. Satcher asked the group who developed *The Call*,
what could be the barriers to "promoting sexual health
and responsible sexual behavior?" The leading barrier
was disparate deeply held beliefs—some propagated by
religious institutions which was painful for those of us in
religious vocations to hear.

The *Call to Action* was to be published in Fall 2000. However, since it was an election year, it was decided to not release the publication until after the election. When George W. Bush, a conservative Republican, was declared president, one of his first actions was to state that there was no such *Call to Action*. Because so many people were involved in the development, it had to be released, but with some negotiated changes. Of those changes the word masturbation was removed in the document.

Dr. Satcher continued to recognize that sexuality and religion are deeply connected and that sexual health in the United States would benefit from leadership from religious groups as well as other agencies with deeply held beliefs relating to sexuality. When he was no longer surgeon general, he held an appointment in Morehouse School of Medicine, Atlanta, GA. There he wrote a Case Statement for the development of an endowed chair in Sexuality and Religion to which I was appointed. On page 1 of this statement he said:

> The integration of sexual health, with mental/emotional, physical, relational, and spiritual health are foundational for the future health of religious institutions and public health in addressing sexual health. Religions contribute decisively to the cultural context for the public understanding of sexuality and sexual health and provide the basis for ethical guidance regarding sexual behavior and expectations.

The training of teachers and religious leaders has become

critical to the accomplishment of the above WHO/WAS sexual rights, which are human rights, and to the Surgeon General's *Call to Action to Promote Sexual Health and Responsible Sexual Behavior*. Educating our religious institutions with proper information and science-based research and knowledge has to be a priority if we are going to be world leaders in developing universal sexual rights for all peoples.

In Mexico City on October 15, 2019, the participants of the 24th World Congress of the World Association for Sexual Health basically reaffirmed the above universal sexual rights for governments and religions with a declaration that affirmed the importance of sexual pleasure. This **Declaration of Sexual Pleasure** states:

"URGE all governments, international intergovernmental and non-governmental organizations, academic institutions, health and education authorities, the media, private sector actors, and society at large, and particularly, all member organizations of the World Association for Sexual Health to:

A. Promote sexual pleasure in law and policy as a fundamental part of sexual health and well-being, grounded in the principles of sexual rights as human rights, including self-determination, non-discrimination, privacy, bodily integrity, and equality;

B. Ensure that comprehensive sexuality education addresses sexual pleasure in an inclusive, evidence-informed and rights-based manner tailored to people's diverse capacities and needs across the life span, in order to allow experiences of informed, self-determined, respectful, and safe sexual pleasure;

C. Guarantee that sexual pleasure is integral to sexual health care services provision, and that sexual health services are accessible, affordable, acceptable, and free from stigma, discrimination, and prosecution;

D. Enhance the development of rights-based, evidence-informed knowledge of the benefits of sexual pleasure as part of well-being, including rights-based funding resources, research methodologies, and dissemination of knowledge to address the role of sexual pleasure in individual and public health;

E. Reaffirm the global, national, community, interpersonal, and individual commitments to recognition of the diversity in sexual pleasure experiences respecting human rights of all people and supported by consistent, evidence-informed policy and practices, interpersonal behavior, and collective action."

The Declarations of Sexual Rights and Sexual Pleasure are profound and call for a transformation of world societies and religions. They are the result of the WHO/WAS response to the spread of unscientific and uninformed sexual information and the high degree of sexual violence, especially to women and youth; and sexual minorities;

unintended pregnancies; sexual diseases; and sexual dysfunction. Members of the WAS knew that there would be governments and religions who would have problems with most of these sexual rights—for example, anything that emphasizes sex as pleasure, homosexuality, transgender issues or any other expression of gender identity, consensual sexual practices, women's choice and access to birth control and services for reproductive health. The rights also include the right to comprehensive sexuality education that is age appropriate, culturally competent and scientifically accurate, as well as the right to marry and/or divorce or to form other types of sexual relationships based on equality. WAS believed that both governments and religions needed to be challenged to address the unhealthy sexual practices in their communities and to propose solutions for developing a sexually healthier world order.

As you read through the "Declaration of Sexual Rights" and the "Declaration of Sexual Pleasure" can you imagine how your church, synagogue, or Mosque would respond to those universal sexual rights? Have you noticed how the declaration for universal sexual rights and sexual pleasure would be more acceptable in Merlin Stone's: *When God was a Woman* world than in a world where sexual knowledge is seen as bad and sex is dirty and sinful? What is the theological framework that could be used to critique sexual health and responsible sexual behavior for all?

Chapter 10

INTEGRATING SEXUALITY, SPIRITUALITY, AND RELIGION

HAVE YOU EVER HAD A DISCUSSION OF SEX AND RELIGION and felt pulled apart internally? Have you ever wondered if you could be sexual and religious at the same time? Have you ever been put in the position where you had to choose between acting out sexually in a safe, fun and experimental way or being religious with your sexual activity limited to marriage and procreation? Have you ever felt spiritual, but not religious? In your religious tradition, if any, did you have positive sexuality education that helped you work through feelings about masturbation, homosexuality, pre-marital sex, or safer sex techniques or were you told what you had to feel?

These are not new questions. Most of them have been asked in one way or another from the beginning of modern religions. It is difficult to be in a conversation about sexuality without religion coming up or in a conversation about religion without sexuality coming up as a topic. The two go together, yet I am told over and over again by religionists, sexologists and lay people that the topics of sexuality and religion are irreconcilable. Certainly my experience, as both a sexologist and a theologian, is that theologians do not trust sexologists, sexologists are suspicious of theologians, and the lay public is totally confused about both fields. In this chapter, we will attempt to address the importance of reconciling these difficult, but important, areas of human experience.

It is my belief that everyone is born both spiritual and sexual, but not religious. Many, however, feel the need to express their spirituality through religion. Both spirituality and religion are ways of finding the meaning of God or love in one's life. The purpose of science is to describe all the various phenomena: behavior, the physical world, and life events. The purpose of spirituality and organized religion is to find meaning to one's behavior, the physical world and life events. Whenever human beings ask questions like: "Who am I?" "Is there purpose to my life?" "What does this experience mean?" "What do I want to do with my life?" "Is there meaning to this world?" "What do I do with my sexual urges?" they are asking spiritual questions. Looking for meaning is a spiritual issue. Whenever a person asks a question of meaning, it is a spiritual question. Religion is made up of the rites and rituals that link one's spirituality to deeply held beliefs and practices.

Everyone is also born sexual, but no one is born a good lover. Sexual response is natural; being a good lover is learned. Did you receive any information or meaning about being a good lover from your religious tradition? This is the dilemma that countless people probably feel all the time. They experience their sexuality, but the meaning they receive from their faith tradition about their sexuality is often not helpful.

Many express their spirituality through deeply held beliefs and/or religious ritual and practices. Science has proven that we are sexual beings throughout our life span. But the purpose of science is only to describe phenomena, and as stated before, the process of looking for meaning has always been a spiritual quest. Throughout history these spiritual questions have led humans to some form of religion, with its special customs, practices, rituals, and, at times, sacred scriptures. It is my contention that one of the goals of life is to integrate one's sexuality and spirituality, one's sexual expression and experience with one's spiritual or religious quest for finding meaning. All too often, however, traditional Abrahamic religions try to separate one's natural sexuality from one's spiritual or religious quest, or/ and set rigid rules about sexual expression, thus creating feelings of alienation, guilt, shame, secretiveness, and even inappropriate and dangerous sexual acting out.

Sexual Value Systems and Religion

As discussed in Chapter 2, there are basically three types of sexual value systems in each of the major religious traditions. The first sexual value system is based on the **Acts of Sex** as being moral or immoral. Persons who hold this sexual value system can find authoritative spokespersons in their religious tradition who hold these views as well as sacred scriptural passages that they believe support their view of sexuality.

The second sexual value system found in the major religious traditions is based on the **Nature of Relationships**. This view holds that human life is all about relationships. It is a human's relationship with self, others, material things, and one's deity as being the most important value. The acts of sex would not define what is moral or immoral, but rather the most important value would be on the motives and consequences of the act. In this view there is nothing intrinsically that is moral or immoral with any of the acts, but rather the person with this sexual value system would weigh the motives and consequences of whether or not the acts of sex enhanced and deepened their relationship with the other. To make these sexual decisions could be helped by knowing what research says, what has been learned from human experience, what good decision-making skills are. Spirituality and Religion should positively inform the sexual decisions.

This sexual value system also has authoritative spokes-persons and their sacred scriptural support. Both sexual value systems are thus supported in the Hebrew Bible, the New Testament (or Christian Bible), the Islamic Holy Qur'an, and the Vedas of Hinduism. While both of the above sexual value systems have scriptural support, the value systems are not complementary or even compatible. Each major religion, individual congregation, and even members of the same family may have persons subscribing to one or the other of these two value systems.

The third sexual value system, also reviewed in Chapter 2, is the one probably held by most people in our world. People holding this sexual value system take from both of the previous value systems based on their own life experience, deeply held beliefs, and comfortability with the particular practice.

The issues around sexuality are so profound, involving the core of one's humanity, that it is extremely important for sexuality education to be a part of each religion's teaching.

All too often, our major religions have abdicated offering good, healthful and helpful comprehensive sexuality education to their children, youth, and adults. The challenges of the 21st century regarding sexuality are such that our major religions need to offer comprehensive science-based sexuality education and guidance if, indeed, our religions are going to promote sexually healthy persons exhibiting responsible sexual behavior. What are these sexual challenges facing religion?

Challenges to Both Sexuality Education and Religion

As discussed in chapters 4, 5, and 6, in my years as a psychologist, theologian, and sexologist, I have become convinced that there is no dichotomy in human development, such as defining male or female, masculine or feminine, heterosexual or homosexual, being single or married, sexually functional or dysfunctional. Each one of these dimensions in human development is on a continuum. Like snowflakes, no two humans are alike in any aspect of being human.

Organized religion, all too often, has taken the "act-based" value system and recognized only heterosexuality as being what nature or God "intended" for all human beings, even though there might be many within that religion that are either "relationship-based" or ambivalent about sexual orientation. Every religion, whether Jewish, Christian, Islam, or Hindu, has homosexual, bisexual, transgender, and heterosexual adherents. There are also associations of gay, lesbian, bisexual, transgender, queer (LGBTQ), and heterosexual supporters within each religious system.

In chapter 7, we learned that in our present day, there are alternative lifestyles. Many of these lifestyles can also be found in the Bible. Khajuraho, the Kama Sutra, and the Vedas of Hinduism also attest to various lifestyles.

In the chapters 4, 5, 6, 7 are all issues that people throughout the world are encountering. They are common modern dilemmas that science is describing that differ from some religions' scriptural and deeply-held beliefs. It is the responsibility of religion to give meaning, understanding and guidance for all these life challenges. Religious systems need helpful, positive sexuality education to bridge experience with meaning so that religious people can make decisions regarding their sexual behavior that do not fall back on guilt and shame instilled by their religion for their choices, and so they will not harm themselves or others in their relationships.

Sexuality Education and Religion

Most of the world religions do not have a formal sexuality education for its adherents. The exception is a few of the Christian denominations. A major study was undertaken by Hartford Seminary and the Lilly Foundation in 2000 (The Hartford Institute for Religion Research, 2000). The study was done with 41 different religious faith communities in the United States, representing 95% of all religious congregations, including Jewish, Roman Catholic, Protestant, Pentecostal, Mormon, Muslim, and Bahai. Only one sexuality-related question was asked and it was only to the Protestants. The question was: "To what extent does your congregation encourage abstaining from premarital sex?" There were 11,000 responses. 22% reported little or no encouragement; 23% reported some; and 55% reported strong encouragement for abstinence until marriage.

According to the U.S. Surgeon General, Dr. David Satcher's *Call to Action to Promote Sexual Health and Responsible Sexual Behavior* (2001), there are few, if any, research studies based on outcomes for religion-based human sexuality programs. It is easier to evaluate the following current programs based on whether or not the program is meeting its goals and objectives related to its professed sexual value system.

There are basically at least three major sexuality education programs that emphasizes the **Acts of Sex** as being moral or immoral. They are Focus on the Family, Sex Respect and True Love Waits. Both teach the spiritual, emotional and physical value of remaining sexually pure until marriage. None cover the range of sexual behaviors. These "abstinence-only until marriage" curricula encourage abstinence from all sexual behaviors. There is an emphasis on failure rates of condom use and safer sexual practices. Books and pamphlets espouse chastity, virginity, abstinence, and other purity practices. Same-sex practices are excluded and may be condemned.

There are two denominationally based curricula that represent the **Relationship-based** sexual value system. The Unitarian Universalist Association (UUA) and the United Church of Christ (UCC) produced a sex education program, Our Whole Lives. This is a comprehensive and progressive curriculum that spans the life cycle and includes justice-oriented traditions of both denominations, including LGBTQ questions and relationships. This curriculum has been successfully field tested for validity and reliability by both denominations.

The Presbyterians, Episcopalians, Lutherans, and United Methodists have curricula that partially emphasize "Relationships," but are silent on some of the important issues, such as masturbation, homosexuality, premarital sex, safer sexual practices, and abortion.

The Roman Catholic Archdiocese of Minneapolis/St. Paul was courageous in promoting a Catholic Coalition for Sexual Minorities, which includes a Catholic Pastoral Committee for Sexual Minorities, a social justice imperative, an ongoing theological dialogue on sexuality, a challenge to its member congregations to love, a vocation to serve God's people, and support of LGBT families by promoting "authentic family values."

In this day when there are so many challenges to sexuality, sexual behaviors, and religion, it is important for the various world religions to develop positive comprehensive sexuality education for its adherents. It is important for the world religions to understand the best in scientific knowledge, research, education, and practices regarding sexuality and sexual behavior. It is also important that the sexologist understand the theology of their religious clients so that they can help their clients find meaning and understanding about their sexuality and sexual behavior that will help them make decisions that are consistent with their religious and sexual values. It is important that persons, of whatever religion, know that within their religious system, there are organizations and leaders that span the various sexual value systems discussed in this chapter. For example, because every religion has gay, lesbian, bisexual and transgender persons within its institution, there are gay, lesbian, bisexual, and transgender organizations within its membership, even though the hierarchy often does not recognize or accept them. There is a yearning from parents looking for faith-affirming ways of explaining and finding meaning to sexuality and sexual behavior for themselves and their children.

The issues about sexuality are complex and not always easy to find meaning. The old and closed views based upon a patriarchal system are no longer relevant or acceptable. Sexuality education within each religious system needs to include the reality of human experience, an understanding of the best science, good sexuality education across the life span, and the teaching of decision-making skills, so that critical sexual decisions can be made in the best interests of the individual, the family, the community, and their faith tradition

The final chapter is an attempt to take all the information from the preceding chapters to build a theology of sinless sex, which can enhance one's spiritual and religious life and experience.

Chapter 11

A THEOLOGY OF SINLESS SEX FOR RELIGIONS

Strange as it may seem, I have always had a love affair with the Bible, both the Hebrew Bible and the Christian Testament (Old and New Testaments, the traditional division of the Bible). I love studying the scriptures. I have on my bookcase behind my desk, on my iPad, and on my desk, at least 34 different English translations of the Bible, one Hebrew/English Torah, two different translations of the Qur'an, and one copy of Hindu Tenants. Even as a sexologist, I think I have spent as much time studying the scriptures as I have reading sexuality journals and books. It is true that besides seminary training, I spent 13 years in pastoral work. I also spent many more years getting doctorates in psychology, theology, and sexology. I have taught about sexuality and religion in numerous seminaries and churches as well as graduate programs in human sexuality. What seems like two very disparate disciplines have always driven my interest in integrating them.

From the previous chapters, you have learned, hopefully, that the Bible is not a sex book and the only sexual relationships that are often described are those involving close relatives, and they were mainly issues around economic and inheritance matters. The main controversial sexual issues in our day involve self-pleasuring, same sex behaviors and relationships, gender transition options, alternative life-styles, non-marital and extramarital relationships, women's rights, and reproductive choice rights. However, I have proposed in this book that sexual morality is based on any sexual behavior among consenting individuals, that is age appropriate, without any pressure or coercion whatsoever, that is not harmful to any participants, and that is out of sight and sound of unwilling observers should be considered normal or acceptable whether or not we choose to do the same behavior. This would be my description of "sinless sex." How, then, do we develop a theology for sinless sex for all religions?

Throughout this book, I have tried to show the negative passages about sexuality that prove to me that taking scriptures literally has been both harmful and impossible. But there are also multitudes of scriptural stories and teachings that lead to justice, moral development and decision-making and sex-positivity. For example, in the Hebrew Bible are many sayings attributed to God, such as, "love your neighbor as yourself" (Leviticus 19:18), "what does the Lord require of you, but to do justly, and to love mercy, and to walk humbly with your God" (Micah 6:8), the Sermon on the Mount (Matthew 5-7), parables found both in the Hebrew Bible and Christian Testament, the Golden Rule (Luke 6:31), and "Beloved, let us love one another, because love is from God; everyone who loves is born of God and knows God. Whoever does not love does not know God, for God is love" (I John 4: 7-8). The Song of Solomon (Song of Songs) is a grand description of erotic love. "How fair and pleasant you are, O loved one, delectable maiden! You are stately as a palm tree, and your breasts are like its clusters. I say I will climb the palm tree and lay hold of its branches. O may your breasts be like clusters of the vine, and the scent of your breath like apples, and your kisses like the best of wine that goes down smoothly, gliding over lips and teeth (Song of Solomon 7: 6-8). The writer is even more explicit. "My beloved thrust his hand into the opening and my inmost being yearned for him. I arose to open to my beloved, and my hands dripped with myrrh" (Song of Solomon 5: 4-5).

The Islamic Q'uran also addresses the importance of love and relationships.

"Allah is with those who are of service to others" (Al Qur'an 29:70), "By Him in Whose Hand my soul is, you will not enter Paradise unless you believe, and you will not believe you love each other...Spread the greetings of peace among you" (Muslim). The Prophet Muhammad(s) said: "Be kind, for whenever kindness becomes a part of something, it beautifies it. Whenever it is taken from something, it leaves it tarnished" (Imam Bukhari's *Book of Muslim Morals and Manners*).

I have several books on my shelves about the Kamasutra or the Art of Eternal Love. "The moment you have in your heart this extraordinary thing called love and feel this depth, the delight, the ecstasy of it, you will discover that for you the world is transformed" (Preface page, Vatsayana's Kamasutra). In the city of Khajuraho, India are the remains of 25 temples devoted to sexuality in diverse sexual formulations: men with men, women with women, men with women, group sex, masturbation, and various positions of sexual play and connection, all within a religious context of worship and ritual (*Khajuraho: Orchha*, by Archana Shankar).

In other words, our various religions' scriptures show how from the beginning, human beings have struggled to know the mind of God. There is a steady progression throughout from a warrior, mean, ruthless, and punishing deity to a God of forgiveness, understanding, sexuality and love. I believe that the evolution of belief and moral understanding of a universal deity (by whatever name) did not stop with the scriptures, but continues to this day through other prophets of religion and the sciences, whether a Martin Luther King, Jr. or a Charles Darwin.

It is my belief that love, spirituality, and sexuality are inextricably bound together. As I have tried to point out in this book, nature's (and/or God's) "intention" is to create persons who are sexual in the fullest sense of the word, which means responsive to sexual pleasuring. This seems to have been true throughout the greater part of primate evolution, non-human, pre-human and human. I truly believe with Genesis 1:31 that "God saw that the Creation was GOOD."

How then do we take all the information in this book and work it into a theology of sexual pleasure or sinless sex that is relevant to daily religious living? The Merriam-Webster Dictionary (2019) defines theology as follows:

The study of religious faith, practice, and experience; especially the study of God and of God's relation to the world.

It should be noted that the word, God, is named differently in different religions, for example, Allah in Islam, as well as by different names even in the Bible, for example, Elohim,

Yahweh, Jehovah, Father, etc. There are several ways of exploring one's experience of God.

One of those ways for Christians is through Jesus' teachings in the Bible. A powerful description of God in the Christian (New) Testament, as I mentioned above, is that "God is Love" as it says in I John 4:7-8. Jesus certainly presented a God of love in his teachings and ministry and he affirmed this when he responded to the Pharisees with "the great commandment" to love God, oneself and others. Love seems to be a central reality in the experience of God and is not abstract or static, but dynamic and active. Whenever we experience complete acceptance from another person or offer unconditional love, we are experiencing God. God's relationship to the world is filled with love and is how humans are to relate to each other.

If we take the last part of this definition of theology, that is, God and God's relation to the world, then it is important to ask: "What is one's experience of God regarding our creation?" One way to experience God or the Divine or the Holy is through the works of God. If all of creation is from God, then we look at nature in awe. Evolution is miraculous. Then we are in touch with the experience of God. I am awed by the nature of our being and our diversity as sexual beings. Our capacity for love and our ability to respond to intimate relationships with deep and meaningful sexual pleasure is a humbling experience. To restrict sexual pleasuring to the procreational function, and to validate sexual pleasure only when it occurs in married heterosexual relationships, diminishes the creative capacities of human beings for expressing their sexuality and offering the giving and receiving of pleasure.

Finally, the experience of God can be discerned whenever humans seek wholeness, that is, to integrate mind, body and spirit. The quest for wholeness and spiritual oneness with God and with each other is experienced in every period of history and among all peoples. When the integration of love, sexuality and spirituality are experienced, God's "intention" is born anew in the world. Sexual pleasuring does not hinder spiritual growth; on the contrary, it has great power to expand it.

The current focus on sexual meaning in our time is a reaction of humans striving to understand the nature of their sexuality. Many are fearful of the implications, one of which may be the discovery that our potential sexual orientation embraces the entire universe and that we can find sexual pleasure in all the dimensions of our life, including self-love, loving others, loving the things in our life, both animate and inanimate, and loving the Thou we serve, whether science, logic, reason, and/or a transcendent deity. That will happen when we join our sexual selves with our spiritual selves and seek appropriate ways of expressing that pleasure in all our relationships. We will then teach the world about sinless sex, which will be a welcome revelation in a world that has been reared on a negative sexual belief system promoting guilt and shame and a dark suspiciousness about even being sexual. My hope is that this exploration of sexuality will be an enhancement to your sexual, spiritual, and religious growth.

And we ourselves know and believe the love which God has for us. God is love, and whoever lives in love lives in union with God and God lives in union with them. (I John 4:16)

References

Buber, M. (1971). *I and Thou* (1st ed.). Touchstone.

Ford, C.S. & Beach, F.A. (1951). *Patterns of Sexual Behavior.* Harper Colophone Books.

Francoeur, R. T. (1991). *Becoming A Sexual Person* (Subsequent ed.). Pearson College.

Greenblatt, S. J. (2017). *How St. Augustine Invented Sex.* New Yorker Magazine, June 19, 2017. https://www.newyorker.com/magazine/2017/06/19/how-st-augustine-invented-sex

Haidt, J. (2013). *The Righteous Mind: Why Good People are Divided by Politics and Religion* (1st ed.). Vintage.

Hartford Institute for Religion Research (2000). www.hartfordinstitute.org.

Joannides, Paul (2015). *Guide to Getting It On!* Goofy Foot Press.

Klein, Fritz (1993). *The Bisexual Option,* 2nd ed. American Institute of Bisexuality, Inc.

Klein, L. K. (2019). *PURE: Inside the Evangelical Movement That Shamed a Generation of Young Women and How I Broke Free* (Reprint ed). Atria.

Kosnik, et al. (1977). *Human Sexuality: New Directions in American Catholic Thought.* This book was commissioned by the Catholic Society of America, later banned and is no longer available.

Lawrence, R. J. (1990). *The Poisoning of Eros: Sexual Values in Conflict.* Augustine Moore Press.

Machacek, D.W. & Wilcox, M.M. (2003). *Sexuality and the World Religions.* ABC/CLIO: Santa Barbara, CA.

Money, J. & Tucker, P. (1976). *Sexual Signatures: On Being a Man Or a Woman.* Little Brown & Co.

Perel, E. (2017). *The State of Affairs: Rethinking Infidelity.* HarperCollins.

Ramachandran, VS (2012). Article by Baldwin, JD & Baldwin, JI in *Encyclopedia of Human Behavior,* (2nd ed). Elsevier: Academic Press.

Rimmer, R. H. (1999). *Thursday My Love.* iUniverse.

Satcher, D. 16th Surgeon General of the U.S. (2001). The Surgeon General's *Call to Action To Promote Sexual Health and Responsible Sexual Behavior.* Office of the Surgeon General, Rockville, MD. http://www.surgeon-general.gov/library.

Shankar, Archana (1997). *Khajuraho: Orchha.* Roli and Janssen, BV.

Stayton, W. R. (1980). *A Theory of Sexual Orientation. Topics in Clinical Nursing,* Vol. 1(4), 1-7.

Stayton, W. R. (1985). *Religion and Adolescent Sexuality. Seminars in Adolescent Medicine,* Vol. 1 (2), 131-135.

Stayton, W. R. (1985). *Alternative Lifestyles: Marital Options. Contemporary Marriage: Special Issues in Couple Therapy.* Dorsey Press.

Stayton, W. R. (1989). *A Theology of Sexual Pleasure*. American Baptist Quarterly, Vol.8 (2), 9-15.

Stayton, W. R. (1992). *Conflicts in Crisis: Effects of Religious Belief Systems on Sexual Health. Religion and Sexual Health*. Kluwer Academic Publications.

Stayton, W. R. (1995). *Religious Belief Systems, Psychotherapy, and Sexual Health. Trends in Health Care, Law & Ethics*, Vol. 10 (3), 7-15.

Stayton, W. R. (1996). *Sexual and Gender Identity Disorders in a Relational Perspective. Handbook of Relational Diagnosis & Dysfunctional Relational Patterns*. Gracewing.

Stayton, W. R. (2007). *Sexual Value Systems and Sexual Health. Sexual Health: Moral and Cultural Foundations*, Vol. 3. Praeger Publishers.

Stayton, W. R. & Pillai-Friedman, S. (2009). *Oh God: The Moral and Scriptural Implications of Sexual Education and Religion. Sexuality Education: Past, Present & Future*, Vol. 1. Praeger Perspectives.

Stayton, W. R. (2018). *Training Religious Leaders in Sexuality Related Issues. Leadership and Sexuality: Power, Principles & Processes*. Edward Elgar Publishing.

Stone, M. (1976). *When God Was A Woman*. Doubleday.

Vatsayana (Date not listed). *Kamasutra*. Singapore.

Acknowledgements

I AM DEEPLY AND PROFOUNDLY APPRECIATIVE FOR THE following:

- Luminare Press of Eugene, Oregon, especially Patricia Marshall, Kim Harper-Kennedy, Melissa Thomas, and Jamie Passaro for guiding me through the publishing process.

- My son, Dr. John Stayton, and his son, Jeremy who were helpful to me in the technical issues of publishing, such as website design and navigating the internet process.

- Sonia Belasco: my Editor, who was so helpful editing, organizing and laying out the structure of this book.

- Dr. David Fletcher (Bucknell University) and Dr. Betsy Crane (Widener University), close friends and colleagues who encouraged me to write this book, supported me through the process, and critiqued every chapter with such invaluable feedback and suggestions.

- Dr. Eli Coleman (University of Minnesota) and Dr. Michele Angello (Widener University) for their important input, feedback and expertise on specific subjects.

- My daughter, Dr. Cheryl Stayton, a terrific researcher, who when all my references were in PA and I was writing in CA, found all my quotes, books, articles, and papers for me.

- Students, family, friends, and therapy clients who have

shared their deeply held stories; some very sad, some outrageously funny, some not shared with anyone else, some very poignant, all of which opened my heart and mind to the tremendous diversity found in human experience.

- My Faith Communities who over many years offered me opportunities to teach my ideas and were a constant source to my own spiritual growth and understanding: Central Baptist Church (Wayne, PA), Oakhurst Baptist Church (Decatur, GA), the Unitarian Universalist Congregation of Susquehanna Valley (Northumberland, PA), and the Unitarian Universalist Congregation of Santa Rosa, CA, all theologically progressive and inclusive additions to their Denominations: American Baptist Churches of the U.S. and the Unitarian Universalist Association.

- Last, but not least to Kathy, my loving spouse and life partner who supported me through this process and read through every word with me in its final submissions.

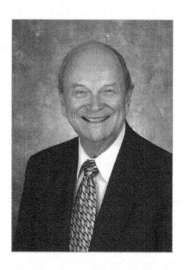

A Brief Biography of
William R. Stayton, MDiv, ThD, PhD

Bill is an ordained minister in the American Baptist Churches of the U.S.A. He is also a licensed psychologist and AASECT certified sexuality educator and therapist. He is a retired Professor at both Widener University Center for Human Sexuality Studies in Chester, PA and the Department of Community Health and Preventive Medicine at Morehouse School of Medicine in Atlanta, GA.

Formerly, Bill was the Executive Director of the Center for Sexuality and Religion, an organization dedicated to facilitating dialogue between the field of sexology and various medical and religious systems. For 28 years, Bill was affiliated with the human sexuality program at the University of Pennsylvania. In 1998, the program moved from the University of Pennsylvania to Widener University in Chester, PA where he was Professor and Director of the graduate programs in Human Sexuality. During his ten years as Director, the program grew from a masters to a doctoral program in human sexuality. He also initiated dual degree programs with both Psychology and Social Work.

He served on the National Advisory Council under the leadership of David Satcher, MD, PhD, 16th U.S. Surgeon General to advance the recommendations set forth in the Surgeon General's *"Call to Action to Promote Sexual Health and Responsible Sexual Behavior"* and then joined the former Surgeon General in the Satcher Health Leadership Institute as Professor at Morehouse School of Medicine to establish an Endowed Chair in Sexuality and Religion. He is also an Adjunct faculty member in the Program on Human Sexuality and on the Advisory Committee at the University of Minnesota School of Medicine. In retirement, Bill teaches courses in the Bucknell University Institute for Lifelong Learning in Lewisburg, PA. He is the author of over 70 journal articles and book chapters on sexuality, religion, theology, sexual orientation, and gender identity/expression. He has been a frequent guest on radio and television programs and has been involved in several documentaries on sexuality.

Bill has been President or Chair of the Board of Directors of: the American Association of Sexuality Educators, Counselors and Therapists (AASECT), the Sexuality Information and Education Council of the U.S. (SIECUS), Planned Parenthood of Southeastern PA, a member of the Board of Directors of the Georgia Campaign for Adolescent Power and Potential from 2011-2017, founded and chaired by actress Jane Fonda. (He remains on the faculty and Advisory Council of the Program in Human Sexuality at the University of Minnesota Medical School.)

Bill has been married with Kathy for 66 years. They have four children: Mark, John, Cheryl, and Paul; five grandsons and two step-granddaughters; and five great-grandchildren. Bill and Kathy split their time between two apartments in Northumberland, PA and Windsor, CA.